PRETTY HANDMADES

FELT & FABRIC SEWING PROJECTS TO
WARM YOUR HEART

LAUREN WRIGHT

Tuva

Tuva Publishing

www.tuvapublishing.com

Address Merkez Mah. Cavusbasi Cad. No:71
Cekmekoy - Istanbul 34782 / Turkey
Tel: +9 0216 642 62 62

Pretty Handmades

First Print 2017 / July

All Global Copyrights Belong To
Tuva Tekstil ve Yayıncılık Ltd.

Content Sewing

Editor in Chief Ayhan DEMİRPEHLİVAN
Project Editor Kader DEMİRPEHLİVAN
Designer Lauren WRIGHT
Technical Editors Leyla ARAS, Büşra ESER
Text Editor Sedef IMER
Graphic Designers Ömer ALP, Abdullah BAYRAKÇI, Zilal ÖNEL
Photograph Stylist Tuba YÜKSEL
Photography Tuva Publishing, Lauren WRIGHT
Illustrations Murat Tanhu YILMAZ

ISBN 978-605-9192-200

Printing House
Bilnet Matbaacılık ve Yayıncılık A.Ş.

f TuvaYayıncılık 🅿 TuvaPublishing
🄴 TuvaYayıncılık 📷 TuvaPublishing

Contents

ABOUT 'PRETTY HANDMADES'

Welcome to 'Pretty Handmades'; a beautiful book of small sewing projects that will delight your senses and inspire you on your sewing journey!

I was beyond thrilled when the opportunity arose to create this book. Not only to showcase all the pretty things that I love making, but more importantly to share with you all the tips and tricks that I have learned in making beautiful handmade things from simple beginnings.

When it came time to design each project, I had so much fun drawing sketches and combining colours and textures with gorgeous fabrics and trims. It was important to me that the projects were not only beautiful but inspiring too. I have tried to combine my love of florals and felt in original ways that showcase a whole range of skills and simple techniques.

My aim has always been to create beginner-friendly patterns with clear step-by-step instructions, without using complicated sewing terms. In 'Pretty Handmades' you can choose from a range of projects such as felt pincushions and softies, fabric mini-quilts, bags, cushion covers and more. These projects cover a variety of techniques such as appliqué, hand embroidery, felt work, patchwork, quilting, and English paper piecing.

The construction techniques are simple and straightforward, yet you can adapt the patterns as you gain confidence and experience. Mix and match different details from the projects, develop your own style, and personalise your projects in a way that tells your own creative story.

It brings me so much joy when I see an idea come to life. There is something so satisfying in just picking up a needle and thread and giving something a go, just for the fun of being creative. To me, it's really about the journey and not the end result. I just try to be creative every day, rather than worrying about things being perfect. It's my hope that the lovely projects in 'Pretty Handmades' inspire you in your journey of making and creating, and give you the confidence to try something different too. I also hope this book encourages you to explore your own creativity and celebrate the gifts and talents you have within you.

Lauren Wright

PROJECT GALLERY

PATCHWORK AND QUILTING TECHNIQUES

Many of the projects in 'Pretty Handmades' are patchworked or pieced and then quilted and bound.

PATCHWORK

Patchwork is the process of sewing small patches of fabrics together. There are so many patchwork techniques but they all have one thing in common: accuracy is paramount. If you use the right tools like a rotary cutter, patchwork ruler and self-healing cutting mat, you're already half-way there! Using a walking foot on your sewing machine is also recommended. It will keep the quilt sandwich together and help avoid puckering.

The patchwork top is the first step in quilting. When the top is complete it's time to make the quilt sandwich!

QUILT SANDWICH

A quilt or quilted project is made up of a quilt sandwich comprised of a piece of backing fabric, then quilt batting or wadding and a patch-worked or pieced quilt top. All three layers are held together with pins, basting stitches, or quilt basting adhesive spray, in preparation for quilting.

QUILTING TECHNIQUES

Quilting is the process of sewing the quilt sandwich together. There are many techniques used for quilting, both on the sewing machine and stitching by hand. The projects in this book use simple quilting styles so that your embroidery or paper piecing are the stars of the show! But feel free to get creative and try any style you like!

Hand Quilting – Hand sewing a running stitch is perfect to highlight special details on your quilted project. You can also use more decorative stitches and details.

Machine Quilting – 'Stitching the Ditch' is an easy way to add definition to quilt blocks. Simply sew in the middle of seam lines to highlight specific fabric panels. You can also sew straight quilting lines like crosshatching to make squares or diamond shapes on your quilt. Free motion quilting is also really popular.

Long Arm Quilting – If you've invested a lot of time and care into sewing a beautiful quilt, you may opt to have it quilted by a long arm quilting machine. With lots of quilting styles and designs to choose from, you might want your piece quilted to highlight special details.

QUILT BINDING

The process of quilt binding can seem a little daunting at first, but it becomes easier with practise and it really is the best way to finish a quilted project. It's the final touch that frames and showcases your work.

Quilts can be bound with premade bias binding, or you can make your own binding.

Picot edge binding is a specialty binding that adds a pretty decorative edge to your sewing. It's also bias cut, so the binding gives nicely around curves and bends.

For straight edged quilts and other projects, you can make your own straight binding.

MAKING QUILT BINDING

Determine the length of the binding required. You'll need enough length to cover all the sides of the quilt. However, you'll need to include extra fabric length for the seam allowance required to sew the fabric strips together and also to overlap the beginning of the binding when stitched to the quilt.

I like to cut 2" (5cm) wide strips for smaller projects. But for larger quilts with a higher-loft polyester wadding, a wider fabric strip of at least 2 ½" (6.5cm) will give you more room to bind the thicker edges of the quilt.

1 Cut strips of fabric from the fabric width using a rotary cutter, clear acrylic patchwork ruler and self healing cutting mat. Be sure to trim off the selvedge at the ends of each strip.

2 Join the strips to create a continuous length of binding, Simply place two fabric strips with right sides together and perpendicular to each other. Line up the raw edges. With an erasable marker, draw a diagonal line from the edge of one strip of fabric to the edge of the other strip of fabric. Pin the fabric together and sew along this line.

3 Trim the corner off the join leaving about a ¼" (6mm) seam allowance.

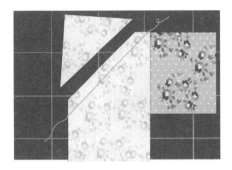

4 Open the seam and press it flat. Continue to sew the strips of fabric together ensuring that the diagonal joins face the same direction.

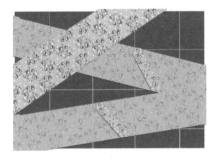

5 When you have joined enough strips fold the fabric strip in half lengthways (wrong sides facing) and press well. You now have a continuous length of binding for your quilt.

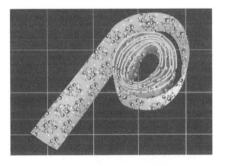

ATTACHING BINDING

6 Create a point at the one end of the binding. Open the folded binding out and fold the right corner down to meet the left hand edge. Press well.

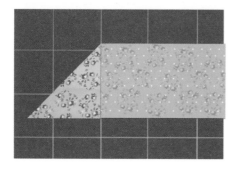

7 Fold the binding back again and press well.

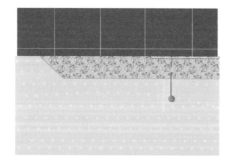

8 Sew the binding to the edge of the base of the quilt. Start at the centre of the base (or the most inconspicuous place to join the binding) and lay the binding along the edge ensuring the raw edges of the binding line up with the raw edges of the quilt. Pin in place. Sew the binding with a ¼" (6mm) seam allowance, starting your stitching about 6" (15cm) from the tip of the binding point. Always back stitch the start and end of your sewing.

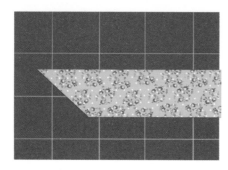

9 When you reach the corner, stop sewing at ¼" (6 mm) from the fabric edge. Pivot your needle and sew directly to the quilt corner. Trim your threads and remove the quilt from the machine.

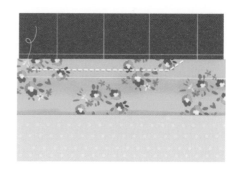

10 Mitre the corner. Fold the binding straight up so that it makes a diagonal fold over the diagonal stitch you placed in the quilt corner. Finger press the fold.

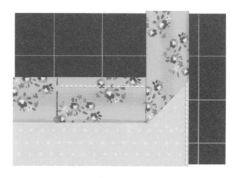

11 Now fold the binding back down so that the top fold sits flush with the edge of the quilt and the raw edges of the binding are placed ready to start sewing the next quilt side. Finger press the fold. Pin the binding in place down this side of the quilt edge.

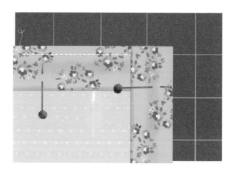

12 Sew the binding down on this side of the quilt, starting at ¼" (6mm) from the top of the quilt. Repeat the same mitring process at the next corner and continue sewing until you are back to the side where you started binding.

13 On this last side, fold the pointed end of the beginning of the binding out of the way. Place the remainder of the binding strip along the quilt edge. Overlap the pointed tail over the top. Place a pin in the left hand binding to mark where the top of the binding point sits above it.

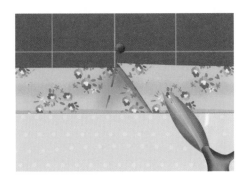

14 Open the left hand section of binding and ensure your pin is still positioned in the same location.

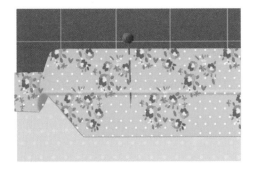

15 Open the pointed tail and turn it so that its right side is perpendicular to the binding. You may need to fold your project so that the two binding edges can meet. Line up the top edge, so that the point is positioned exactly where the pin is placed in the binding. Remove that pin and then pin the two strips of fabric together.

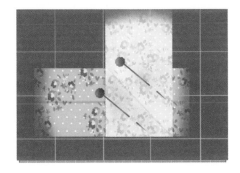

16 The fold line on the binding (from the point) acts as a seam marker. Sew the fabric along this line. Trim off the extra fabric on each side of the seam (leaving a ¼" (6 mm) seam allowance).

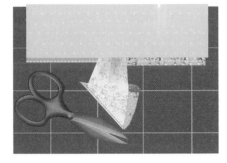

17 Finger press this seam open.

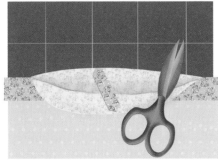

18 Lay the quilt flat. The binding join will sit neatly down the edge of the quilt. You may wish to press the binding flat.

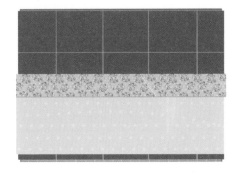

19 It is now time to sew the remainder of the binding seam.

20 When finished, fold the binding over towards the back of the quilt. Pin or clip the binding in place.

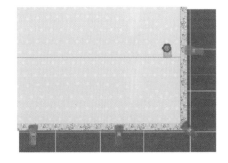

21 Using a single strand of 60 weight bobbin thread, blind stitch the binding to the back of the quilt with small, fine stitches. See the Stitch Library for more details on blind stitching. Mitre the corners as you go.

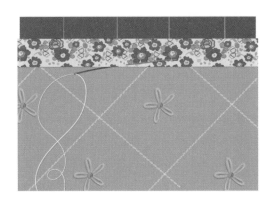

WORKING WITH FELT

If you're going to spend your precious time stitching up something special, you want it to last. Be sure to honour your work, by using the best materials you can afford.

For all projects in this book, I recommend using 100% merino wool felt. It's more expensive than other forms of felt. But if you're only creating small projects and you'd like your sewing to last, then 100% wool felt is such a beautiful medium and it really makes a difference to the look and feel of every piece you'll make. It will last longer, and keep its shape better. It's strong and durable. It's less likely to pill or bobble, so it's great for hand-making toys or pincushions. It cuts well, doesn't fray like fabric and can be easily shaped and moulded. Wool also has a natural resistance to staining, fire, water and mildew, so it's great for those projects that you really can't clean by throwing them in the machine.

If you can't source 100% wool felt, try a felt blended with rayon. Wool blend felt can sometimes be easier to source. If your local sewing or quilting supply store doesn't stock wool felt, try online.

TIPS FOR CARE

You can iron 100% wool felt if you need to. Just use a wool heat setting and cover the felt with a press cloth so you don't damage the wool fibres.

Don't use wool felt on a project you wish to machine wash. Wool felt and washing machines don't mix! Dry cleaning is your first option. Spot cleaning wool felt is also recommended. If dry marks don't brush off, use a damp cloth to gently dab away at them. Don't rub the felt, or add soaps or cleaning products.

CUTTING FELT

The best way to ensure you have a beautiful felt creation, is to be careful when you're cutting. Precision and accuracy is the key. Use small sharp scissors with a short blade and pointed tip to get a neat finish and those wonderfully crisp edges.

TRANSFERRING DESIGNS

When cutting shapes from a pattern, there are several methods you can use. The most popular by far, is to trace your template onto 'freezer paper'.

THE FREEZER PAPER METHOD

1 Copy or trace your template onto the paper side of the freezer paper.

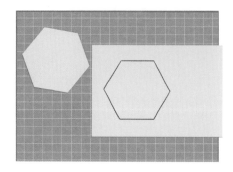

2 Roughly cut around each template piece and lay it on the felt.

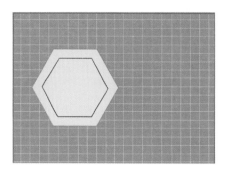

3 Using a warm iron, run it over the paper side of the template. The heat will help the plastic underside of the freezer paper to adhere to your felt.

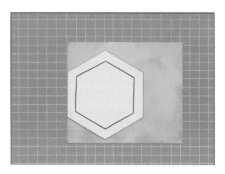

4 Cut out the template pieces on the drawn line and then simply peel the paper away. It comes away easily and leaves no residue.

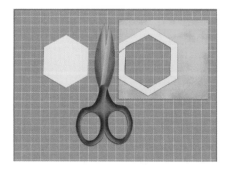

5 Keep the freezer paper templates as these can be reused a number of times.

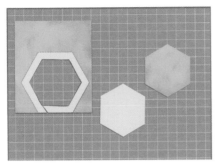

Please note that this method is best suited to wool felt. Test a small area of your felt with the iron and paper before commencing. Be sure to cover your felt with a press cloth (or scrap piece of cotton fabric) so as not to damage the felt (especially if it is not 100% wool).

THE PAPER TEMPLATE METHOD

Traditional paper templates can also be effective.

1 Don't cut the paper template out on the line before you start, but leave a small border around the template edge. Pin the paper template to your felt.

2 Cut out your shape on the drawn line.

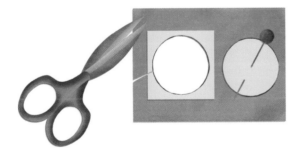

3 If you need to cut more than one shape from the same template, use the piece of felt you just cut as a template, rather than the paper. You're more likely to get more uniform shapes that way.

TRANSFERRING EMBROIDERY DETAILS TO FELT USING TISSUE PAPER

It's often difficult to trace embroidery details onto coloured felt. So I prefer to use the Tissue Paper Method.

1 Trace the embroidery designs and individual details onto a small piece of thin tracing or tissue paper.

2 Pin the paper over the felt shape, making sure all the details line up.

3 Sew the embroidery details onto the felt by stitching directly through the paper.

4 When you've finished the embroidery, hold the stitches with one hand as you gently tear away the paper with the other. Use your needle to help tease any stray bits of paper out from under the stitches (if necessary).

HAND SEWING FELT

As with all sewing, practice makes perfect. When sewing felt, be careful about your stitch size, length and consistency. If you're not happy with the finish of your stitching, don't be afraid to pull it out and start over. Wool felt can be very forgiving like that!

STITCH LIBRARY

There are so many different hand sewing stitch types with so many uses. You'll come to find that they are often named differently, depending on where you find yourself in the world. You'll find that the construction of each stitch can also vary depending on how you were taught and whether you are right or left handed.

Here's a brief description of some of the more common stitches, what they're used for and how to sew them.

BACK STITCH

Back stitch is the perfect choice for quick and easy embroidery outlines because it creates a solid looking line.

Bring the thread up from the back of the fabric at point 1 and take one stitch backward down through point 2. Bring the needle up one stitch length in front (point 3), then stitch back into point 1. Continue back stitching in this way, ensuring the stitch lengths remain the same.

BASTING STITCH

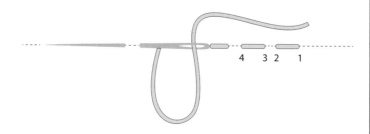

Basting stitch holds fabrics together temporarily, while other sewing is completed. Use large running stitches to baste fabric or felt in place. These stitches should be easy to remove when the project is complete, so are often sewn with a single strand of thread in a contrasting colour that's easy to see.

BLANKET STITCH

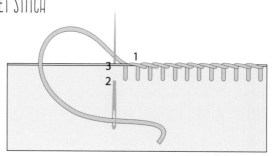

Blanket stitch creates a decorative and protective finish on fabric edges. It's ideal for sewing felt together and for appliqué.

On a raw fabric or felt edge, sew a single stitch from under the fabric at point 1 and around the raw edge. Bring the thread back up though point 1, tuck it under the first stitch and insert the needle at point 2. Catch the floss under the needle as you pull the needle out at point 3. Pull firmly and repeat this step to continue.

BLIND STITCH

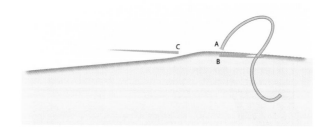

These small, fine stitches are great for hemming and are used throughout this book for securing quilt binding.

Hide the knot on the underside of the binding. Bring the thread up through the binding (very close to the binding edge). Sew a small stitch over the binding edge and insert the needle, coming out again a few mm further on. Repeat this series of stitches, ensuring that the thread cannot be seen from the front of the quilt. Keep the stitch length consistent.

FRENCH KNOT

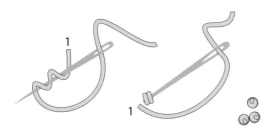

French knots are small dots which are great for showcasing details, like the seeds on a strawberry or the eyes on a small doll.

Bring the thread out at the required position at point 1. Hold the eye of the needle on the fabric near the thread starting point. Encircle the thread twice around the needle, manoeuvre the needle tip to the starting point, and reinsert it a thread or two beside point 1. Pull the thread through to the back, holding it firmly as you do. Larger knots can be made by increasing the numbers of floss strands on the needle or the number of times the floss is wound around the needle.

LAZY DAISY STITCH

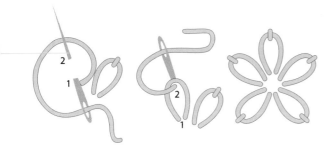

Lazy daisy stitch is ideal for sewing pretty flower shapes. Sew each lazy daisy stitch around a central point like a French knot to create a flower.

Bring the thread out at point 1. Hold the thread and then insert the needle back into point 1 and then back out at point 2. Pull the thread through but keep it under the needle point, to form a loop. Fasten the loop by sewing a small stitch over the loop from point 2. Repeat the stitch five times to make a daisy flower shape. Use a French knot to form the centre of the daisy.

RUNNING STITCH

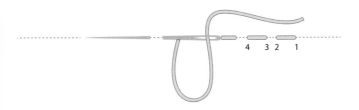

The most basic of hand stitching techniques, running stitch, is a series of straight stitches sewn in a line. It's often used as a simple but effective hand quilting technique.

Bring the needle up from the fabric back at point 1, and push it down at point 2. Continue to pass the needle over and then under the fabric, in a straight line. Adjust the stitch length to change the effect of the quilting.

SATIN STITCH

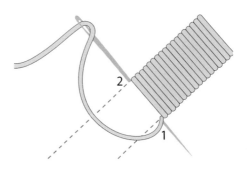

Satin stitch is used to fill small spaces with solid colour. It is made up of straight stitches worked closely beside each other in a parallel fashion. Sew a straight stitch from 1 to 2, and then repeat this stitching to fill the space.

WHIP STITCH

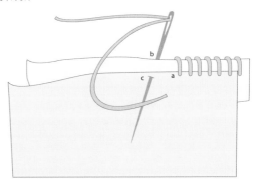

Whip stitch is ideal for edging or sewing fabrics like felt together around the raw edge. It's also a useful alternative when an area is too small for blanket stitch.

Hold the aligned raw edges of the felt together. From the wrong side of the felt, push the needle through the first layer to exit at point A. Loop the thread around the raw edge and in at point B, (directly behind point A). Angle the needle sideways to come out at point C. Again, loop the thread over the raw edge and in at point D and out at point E. Continue the stitches, ensuring they are parallel and not angled.

YOUR SEWING AND CRAFT TOOL BOX

You may have been sewing for a long while, and have a whole arsenal of essential and clever tools for sewing and crafting. But if you're just starting out, it's difficult to know which pieces will be really beneficial. Generally speaking, you get what you pay it's wise to invest in the right tools. If you spend a lot of time sewing something precious, then it makes sense to value your time and your work and use the best tools and materials you can.

Here is a list to get you started. These items have all been used in making the projects in this book. Some are must have items. Others will help you improve the look and feel of your finished pieces, so are well worth the investment.

TOOLS AND NOTIONS

SEWING THREAD for your sewing machine, in a range of colours. Neutrals are a great option to blend in well with varying fabric colours.

SIX STRANDED EMBROIDERY FLOSS
Choose the best thread for your project, like cotton embroidery floss from DMC. It's readily available and comes in a huge array of colours. The skeins of floss or thread are made up of six strands, which you can separate according to the needs of your project. Two or three strands of floss work really well for embroidery and felt work. But which thread colour do you choose? I love to coordinate my thread with my felt colour. If you can't get an exact match, choose a thread colour that is a shade darker than your felt or fabric. Or select a contrasting shade to really stand out!

SEWING PINS in varying lengths and with shanks of varying widths. You'll use pins for all sorts of projects, so you'll need a wide range.

SEWING NEEDLES for various purposes including general sewing and embroidery. Be sure to choose the right sized needle. Large needles can leave holes in your work, so choose a needle that accommodates your thread type, but also treats your fabric or felt well too. Embroidery and milliners needles are great for the projects in this book. They have longer eyes so they can fit more strands of floss through them. But they're also long and narrow, so they're perfect for sewing hexagons, stitching binding on a quilt, or embroidering a pretty design.

PINCUSHION
A pretty pincushion is essential. You'll be using it a lot! If you don't already have one, make yourself a Flower Friends Pincushion (one of the lovely projects included in the book).

SCISSORS
• Large heavy shears with long blades are great for fabric.
• Small scissors with short, sharp blades are perfect for cutting felt.
• Embroidery scissors with thin blades, are small and fine for snipping floss.
• Keep your old craft scissors for paper!

ROTARY CUTTER with a retractable blade, patchwork ruler made from transparent acrylic, and a large self healing cutting mat to accommodate large pieces of fabric.

TAPE MEASURE AND STEEL RULER with both metric and imperial measurements. The steel ruler is terrific when accuracy is crucial, as tape measures can stretch over time.

PENS AND MARKERS
Some of the options you may wish to use include;
• Ball point pen for tracing felt embroidery details on tracing paper.
• Lead pencil for tracing designs on the paper side of fusible webbing.
• Water or heat erasable marker for marking details on fabric, like tracing embroidery designs.
• Iron-on transfer pens are great for transferring traced embroidery designs to fabric (note that these designs will be reversed during the transfer process).

THIMBLES to protect your fingers while hand sewing. I love leather and silicon thimbles and finger covers.

BODKIN or safety pin for threading ribbon or elastic through fabric casings.

SEAM RIPPER OR QUICK-UNPICK. You never know when you may need one!

QUILTING CLIPS like Wonderclips. These are a wonderful alternative to pins and terrific to use on materials that cannot be pinned (like vinyl).

QUILT BASTING OR ADHESIVE SPRAY to secure wadding when making your quilt sandwich.

SPRAY STARCH to give your fabrics a crisp and clean finish.

PAPER BACKED FUSIBLE HEAT BONDING WEB like Vliesofix or Easyfix for appliqué. There's more details about its use for appliqué in the 'Appliqué Techniques' section.

FREEZER PAPER FOR QUILTING. This is a must-have tool for transferring designs to felt. It's super easy to use too! See full instructions for using freezer paper in the 'Working With Felt' section.

TIMBER EMBROIDERY HOOPS in various sizes. These are great to keep your embroidery stitches even. They also make a lovely 'frame' for displaying your handiwork.

IRON AND IRONING BOARD. Keep both immaculately clean and well cared for. It's so important to press your fabrics at each stage in construction. It will provide your pieces with the best possible finish.

EMBELLISHMENTS like buttons, bows, ribbons, lace, pom pom trim, crochet lace trim, leather tags and patches, crochet embellishments, embroidered braid and printed cotton tape, can make all the difference to the finish of a completed project.

MATERIALS

QUILTER'S WEIGHT 100% COTTON FABRIC is a medium weight fabric that is typically used for quilting and small sewing projects. It's strong and durable and also comes in a huge array of colours and prints.

LAWN is a finely woven cotton fabric with a higher thread count. This creates a fine, light weight fabric with a beautifully textured feel. Liberty of London specialises in lawn, and many of the projects in this book showcase this gorgeous fabric.

LINEN FABRIC in natural shades creates the perfect backdrop for highlighting special fabric prints and delightful florals. Often blended with cotton, it is a popular choice for modern quilting and sewing projects.

QUILT BATTING OR WADDING creates the padding inside a quilt. It's placed between the fabric top and bottom of the quilt to form a 'quilt sandwich.' Cotton and bamboo batting are ideal, but polyester quilt batting can be more affordable. When making mini quilts, and other small sewing projects, I prefer the fusible types like Pellon Vilene.

WOOL FELT. 100% merino felt is more expensive but well worth the investment. Read more about felt in the 'Working With Felt' section.

QUILT BINDING. Purchase pre-made double fold bias binding, including picot edge binding for a decorative finish. Or make your own continuous straight or bias binding from your favourite fabrics. For more details, see the section on 'Patchwork and Quilting Techniques'.

APPLIQUÉ TECHNIQUES

MATERIALS REQUIRED

- Template of shape to appliqué

- Cotton fabric scraps for your appliqué shapes and base fabric to appliqué onto (100% cotton is recommended)

- Paper backed fusible heat bonding web like Vliesofix or Easyfix

- Ball Point Pen

- Scissors

- Iron and ironing board

- Embroidery floss and needle to hand stitch the appliqué OR sewing machine with complimentary thread colours

HOW TO APPLIQUÉ

1 Trace the template pieces onto the paper side of your fusible web. Remember that your appliqué will be a mirror image of your template. So trace in reverse (if it hasn't already been reversed for you).

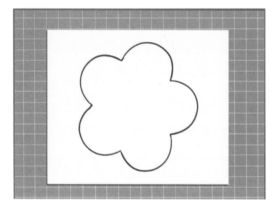

2 Roughly cut around each traced piece of fusible web ensuring you leave a small border (do not cut out your design on the line).

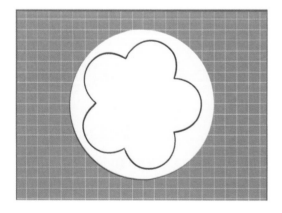

3 Place the fusible web pieces onto the wrong side (the back) of your chosen fabrics so that your template (the paper side) is facing you and the webbing is between the paper and the fabric. Fuse the paper to the fabric with a hot steam-free iron.

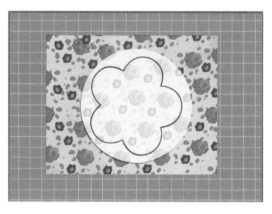

4 Cut out each appliqué piece by neatly cutting on your traced lines.

5 Peel the backing paper off each appliqué piece and position them neatly on your project base fabric. Use your template as a placement guide for overlapping or layering the individual pieces.

6 Secure the appliqué with a hot iron.

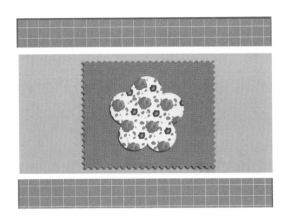

7 Appliqué around your fabric shapes. You may choose to hand stitch or machine stitch around the raw fabric edges of your design. Blanket stitch, satin or blind stitch are all popular. The 'Stitch Library' has extra details on stitch types and techniques.

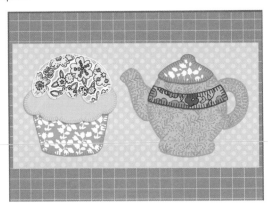

8 Stitch the 'bottom' layers of the fabric design first. Stitch the top-most pieces of fabric last. I prefer to use blanket stitch as it gives each fabric piece a lovely border and it nicely protects the raw edges of the fabric.

ENGLISH PAPER PIECING TECHNIQUES

English paper piecing is a traditional sewing technique that is very popular right now. It's a wonderful thing too, as it's great for using up fabric scraps. And we all have too many of those! Fabric is stitched around paper shapes, which are then tessellated together in different combinations. These templates come in all sorts of shapes and sizes, like hexagons (or hexies), jewels, kites, triangles, diamonds, elongated hexagons, squares, and half hexagons.

The instructions below explain the process of making and joining hexagon shapes using the glue basting method (which I find quicker and easier than stitch basting).

MATERIALS

• Paper templates in varying sizes and shapes.

• Glue basting pen designed specifically for paper piecing.

• Fabric scraps.

• Scissors.

• Milliner's needle – size 9 (thin, long, sharp needle, with a longer eye).

• 60 weight polyester bobbin thread (or a similar fine thread) in a neutral colour like grey, beige or white. Fine, neutral coloured threads ensure your stitches are less likely to be seen.

• Iron and ironing board.

HOW TO GLUE BASTE HEXAGONS

1 Place your hexagon paper on the wrong side of your fabric and hold in place. Roughly cut around the hexagon shape leaving at least a ¼" (6mm) seam allowance.

2 Using a glue pen, run a small amount of glue along the edge of one side of the hexagon paper (being careful not to use too much glue, or to glue too close to the edge of the paper).

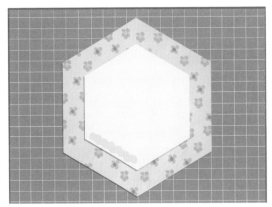

3 Fold the fabric over firmly and secure.

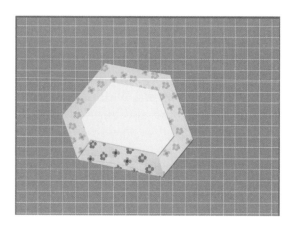

4 Glue the second side and then fold it over, including the edge of the first side.

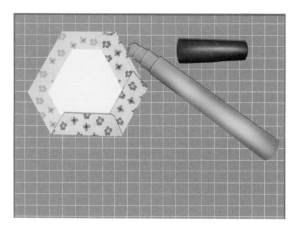

5 Repeat this process to fold over all six sides of the fabric.

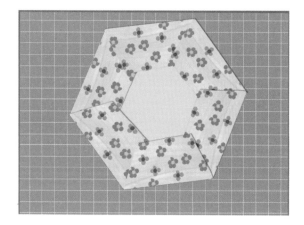

Be especially careful to keep the fabric folded firmly near the points or corners.

6 Repeat this process until you have made the quantity of hexagons (or other shapes) required for your project.

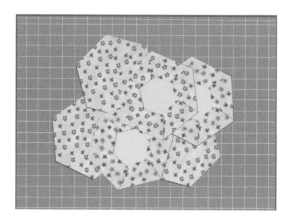

HOW TO SEW HEXAGONS TOGETHER

7 Choose two hexagons, and identify the sides to be joined. Hold them right sides together, being sure to line up the edges and corners of the side you wish to sew.

8 Thread your fine needle with a single strand of fine thread and knot one end. When you start, sew a couple of stitches in the same place to secure the start of your stitching. Use very fine and small whip stitches to sew the two sides of the hexagons together. Start at one corner and stitch along the edge to the next corner.

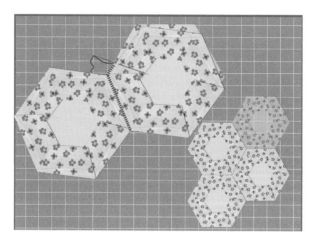

As you stitch, catch 2 - 3 threads from the folded edge of both pieces of fabric, being careful not to stitch through the actual paper.

9 When you finish sewing that edge, secure your stitching with a couple of stitches repeated in the same place at the end of your hexagon side. This keeps the stitches tight and the seams (for each side of the hexagon) neatly intact. Next, fold the hexagons out flat and identify the next hexagon to be added to the design.

10 Repeat the method described above to join all the hexagons together in your chosen design. You will find that you can join many sides together with one single strand

of thread, if you sew them continuously. You can also run your needle and thread up the back of the seam stitches (on the wrong side of the hexagon) to move the thread to another spot to start stitching a new seam. But at times the only option will be to secure your stitching with a few back stitches on the wrong side of your hexagon, cut your thread and then start your sewing again at a new place. You'll discover you need to fold the hexagons at various times in order to stitch certain sides together.

11 When all the shapes are sewn together, you can begin removing the papers. Remove the papers from the centre of the design first and then work your way out to the edges. Carefully remove the papers by lifting up the fabric on one side of the back of the hexagon and sliding your finger along to tease the fabric from the glue. When you find the corner of the paper, you can carefully manoeuvre the rest of the paper out.

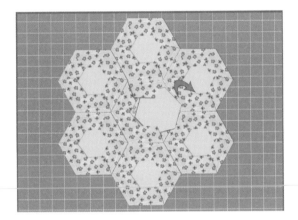

12 You may like to press the back of each hexagon with a warm iron as you go. This will help the hexagons retain their shape.

Projects

Honey Hive Stitchy Book

The Honey Hive Stitchy Book is perfect for
sewing on the go. Pop in your embroidery scissors,
add some floss cards to the pocket, store your sewing pins in
the hive shaped pincushion and your needles on the felt tabs.
Practical and pretty, you can customise the layout to suit your
own sewing needs. It's beautifully decorated with felt flowers
and stitchy details. Make the matching Busy
Bee Pincushion to create
the perfect pair of sewing
accessories.

Finished Size
Approximately 6 ½" (16.5cm)
wide at the base and 7 ¼"
(18.4cm) tall.

✓ 18" (46cm) x 22" (56cm) fat quarter of floral quilter's cotton for the binding

✓ Four 9" (23cm) squares of natural coloured linen

✓ Two 9" (23cm) squares of medium weight fusible fleece

✓ Two 9" (23cm) squares of medium weight fusible interfacing

✓ 3" (7.6cm) square of floral quilter's cotton for bee hive door

✓ Three 1 ½" (4cm) squares of print quilter's cotton for the ½" hexagon detail

✓ Paper backed fusible appliqué bonding web like Vliesofix

✓ Freezer paper

✓ 5" (12.7cm) square of mid pink wool felt for the front cover bee hive

✓ 2" (5cm) square of mid pink wool felt for the bee hive pincushion door

✓ 4" (10cm) square of pale pink wool felt for the bee hive pincushion

✓ 5" (12.7cm) x 1 ¾" (4.5cm) of white wool felt

✓ Two 4 ½" (11.4cm) x 1 ½" (4cm) pieces of wool felt in apricot and pale green

✓ 4 ½" (11.4cm) x ⅜" (1cm) piece of wool felt in pale pink

✓ Scraps of wool felt for the leaves in pale green and mid green

✓ Scraps of wool felt for the flowers in white, deep pink, mid pink, pale pink and apricot

✓ Scraps of wool felt for the bees in white, beige, peach and green

✓ DMC floss in Ecru, B5200 (white), 3790 (ultra dark beige grey), 3348 (light yellow green), 3779 (ultra very light terra cotta), 602 (mid cranberry), 352 (light coral)

✓ 2" (5cm) x ½" (12mm) leather label or other trim for decorating the back cover

✓ 6" (15.2cm) of ⅜" (1cm) wide natural coloured cotton crochet lace trim

✓ 4 ½" (11.4cm) of ⅝" (1.5cm) wide natural coloured cotton crochet lace trim

✓ 23" (58.4cm) of 1/16" (1.5mm) wide satin ribbon

✓ Water erasable pen

✓ Honey Hive Stitchy Book templates

✓ Thick paper to create hexagon shapes

✓ Glue basting pen

✓ 60 weight polyester bobbin thread in white, grey or beige

✓ Milliner's needle in size 9

✓ Pinking shears or zig zag scissors (optional)

✓ Four ⅝" (1.5cm) diameter decorative buttons

✓ Polyester hobby fill

✓ Appliqué glue (optional)

✓ Quilting clips

✓ Press cloth or cotton fabric scrap

✓ Rotary cutter, ruler and mat

✓ General sewing supplies

INSTRUCTIONS

TIP: For help with the different stitch types used in this project, please see the 'Stitch Library'. Visit the 'Appliqué Techniques' section for more detailed appliqué information. The 'Working With Felt' section has lots of handy tips for sewing with wool felt.

MAKE THE FELT FLOWERS

1 Make four small felt flowers, one large felt flower and five felt leaves to adorn the stitchy book. You will need scraps of pale pink, mid pink, deep pink and apricot to sew the four small flowers. They are the same as those in the Polly Plaits project, so follow steps 18 and 19 to make one in each colour using the provided template. Use the freezer paper to cut out five small leaves; three in pale green and two in mid green.

2 Use white felt scraps and follow the instructions in steps 34 – 38 of the Busy Bee Pincushion project to construct the white flower. Set the flowers and leaves aside.

ASSEMBLE THE FOUR LINEN BOOK PAGES

3 Centre the template of the curved book shape on the front of each of the four 9" (23cm) squares of linen, then trace the outline.

4 Following the manufacturer's instructions, secure the 9" (23cm) squares of fusible fleece onto the wrong side of two 9" (23cm) squares of linen. Then secure the 9" (23cm) squares of fusible interfacing onto the remaining two 9" (23cm) squares of linen. Set aside.

MAKE THE FRONT COVER

5 Prepare the bee hive applique shape, following the instructions in the Applique Techniques section.

6 Prepare the bee hive door applique shape, making sure to add a small border around the door curve, as shown by the dashed line on the template.

7 Using the template as a guide, position the felt bee hive on a fusible fleece backed square of linen. Tuck the fabric door under the bee hive so that the base of the door and the bee hive are aligned. Press in place.

8 Use three strands of light yellow green floss to blanket stitch the raw fabric edge along the base of the bee hive door.

9 Using a water erasable marker, draw in the bee hive stitching lines as indicated on the template.

10 Use three strands of terra cotta floss to sew a running stitch along these lines and around the inside edge of the entire bee hive shape. Remove the lines on the bee hive with a damp cloth.

11 Follow the instructions outlined in steps 11, 12 and 14 of the Busy Bee Pincushion project to appliqué and stitch the felt bee on the top right hand side of the bee hive. Use white, beige and peach felt scraps, and white and beige grey floss. Mark the bee's flight line with a water erasable marker, using the template as a guide for placement. Stitch the flight line using three strands of light coral floss and a fine running stitch. Remove the lines with a damp cloth.

12 Position the white and mid pink flower on the bottom left hand side of the bee hive with two green leaves. Place the apricot small flower and leaf on the bottom right hand side. Stitch each flower and leaf in place using matching sewing thread. Be sure to position them at least a ¼" (6mm) from the edge of the traced stitchy book template. This seam allowance will be required for the binding.

13 Trim around the outside of the cover on the drawn line. Set aside.

MAKE THE INSIDE LEFT PAGE

14 The inside left page will be made using one of the linen squares lined with the medium weight interfacing. Centre the 4 ½" (11.4cm) x 1 ½" (4cm) piece of apricot wool felt about 1" (2.5cm) up from the straight base of the template. Pin in place. Use three strands of terra cotta floss and a small running stitch to sew the two short sides and along the base. Then also sew a line down the centre to form two pockets.

15 Hand stitch the pale pink small flower and mid green leaf to the bottom left corner of the pocket (being sure to leave at least a ¼" (6mm) seam

allowance from the outside edge of the drawn template).

16 Pin the 4 ½" (11.4cm) x 1 ½" (4cm) piece of pale green wool felt about 1" (2.5cm) up from the top of the apricot pocket. Machine stitch the top edge of the green felt in place. Use pinking shears or other decorative scissors to trim the base of the green felt if you wish.

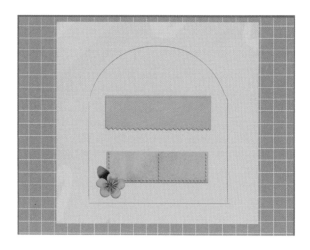

17 Centre the 4 ½" (11.4cm) x ⅜" (1cm) strip of pale pink wool felt over the 4 ½" (11.4cm) piece of 5/8" (1.5cm) wide natural coloured lace trim. Use appliqué glue or pins to hold it in place as you machine sew the pieces together with a straight stitch around the inside edge of the pink felt.

18 Position the lace strip over the top of the green felt and pin in place. Sew a decorative button at each end to secure the strip in place.

19 Place a mark ¾" (2cm) on either side of the centre point of the pink felt strip. Hand sew a few small stitches (using terra cotta floss) through the felt and backing fabric to divide the strip into three sections.

20 Mark a spot in the centre of the top of the linen, about 1" (2.5cm) above the pink felt and lace strip. Cut an 11" (28cm) piece of narrow 1/16" (1.5mm) wide ribbon and heat seal the ends to prevent fraying. Use a few well placed hand stitches to sew the centre of the strip of ribbon in place over the mark. (This ribbon will hold the scissor handles in place when a pair of small embroidery scissors is placed through the centre of the pink felt and lace strip.)

21 Use a water erasable pen to trace the dashed curvy flight line from the template onto the fabric. Stitch in running stitch with three strands of Ecru floss. Remove traced lines with a damp cloth.

22 Trim around the outside of the fabric on the traced line. Set aside.

MAKE THE INSIDE RIGHT PAGE

23 Following steps 5 and 6 on the previous page, prepare the bee hive shape and bee hive door, using pale and mid pink wool felt.

24 Trace the bee hive door onto freezer paper and roughly cut out. Be sure to add a small ¼" (6mm) border around the bee hive door curve (for overlapping). Press the door template onto the 2" (5cm) square of mid pink wool felt, cut it out on the line and peel off the freezer paper.

25 Using three strands of terra cotta floss, sew a running stitch around the top curve of the door (sewing the two layers of felt together as you go). Next mark the bee hive stitching lines on the felt, using a water erasable marker.

26 Sew a running stitch along these lines. Then remove the water erasable lines.

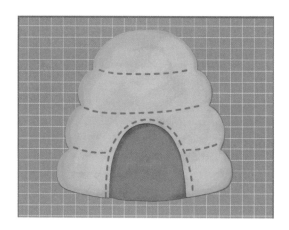

27 Using the template as a guide, position the bee hive onto the remaining piece of linen backed in fusible fleece. It should be centred 2 ½" (6.3cm) from the base of the drawn template. Pin in place.

28 Use three strands of terra cotta floss to sew a running stitch around the outside edge of the bee hive shape from the base of one side of the bee hive door and up around to the other side. Leave the base of the door open and add a small amount of hobby fill to stuff the bee hive into a padded pincushion.

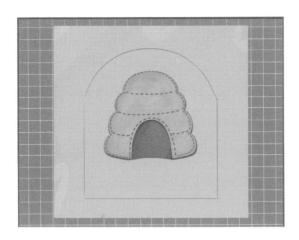

29 Stitch the bee hive door closed.

30 Pin or appliqué glue the 6" (15.2cm) of ⅝" (1cm) wide crochet lace trim to the top of the 5" (12.7cm) x 1 ¾" (4.5cm) piece of white wool felt, folding the excess at each end towards the back. Position the felt just below the bee hive and sew in place. Trim the base of the white felt using pinking shears or decorative scissors if you wish.

31 Sew the remaining two decorative buttons onto the ends of the lace. Then sew the deep pink small felt flower and leaf onto the right hand side of the bee hive base (using the template as a placement guide).

32 Appliqué a bee to the left side of the bee hive, using white, beige and pale green felt. Use the instructions outlined in steps 11, 12 and 14 of the Busy Bee Pincushion project to create the bee with beige grey floss. However,

MAKE THE BACK COVER

35 Use the template provided to trace and cut three ½" hexagon shapes from heavy paper.

36 Glue baste three hexagons onto the paper shapes using the three 1 ½" (4cm) squares of print fabric. For more detailed instructions on making and joining hexagons, see the 'English Paper Piecing Techniques' section at the beginning of the book.

37 Arrange the hexagons like the template shape and whip stitch the sides together using 60 weight bobbin thread and a milliner's needle.

38 Remove the piecing papers and press.

39 Trace around the outside of the hexagon shape onto the paper side of the fusible appliqué bonding web. Cut out the shape about 1/8" (3mm) in from the drawn line. Follow the manufacturer's instructions and use a warm iron to secure the bonding web to the wrong side of the hexagon shape. Peel off the backing paper.

40 Use the template as a guide to position the hexagon detail on the last remaining piece of linen (backed with fusible interfacing). Press in place with a warm iron. Use a single strand of bobbin thread to blind stitch around the outside edge of the hexagon shape. Then use three strands of Ecru floss to quilt a running stitch about 1/16" (1.5mm) from the edge of the hexagon detail.

41 Trace the flight line with an erasable marker then sew a running stitch over the line using three strands of mid cranberry floss.

42 Position a leather label on the centre top of the linen shape. Use terra cotta floss to stitch in place.

43 Trim around the template shape.

ASSEMBLE THE STITCHY BOOK PAGES

44 Pin or clip the Inside Right Page and Back Cover together with wrong sides facing. Sew a scant ⅛" (3mm) seam around the outside edge of the two pieces to join them together.

45 Repeat previous step for the Front Cover and Inside Left Page.

46 Cut the remaining piece of narrow 1/16" (1.5mm) wide ribbon in half so that you have two 6" (15.2cm) lengths. Heat seal each end. Use a few small stitches to secure one piece of ribbon on the left hand side of the inside left page (as marked on the template). Stitch the other piece of ribbon in place on the right hand side of the Inside Right Page.

47 Create a continuous length of bias cut binding for the outside edge of the stitchy book pages. Cut the binding fabric into 2" (5cm) strips, by cutting on the bias on the fat quarter (from the top left hand corner to the bottom right hand corner). You will need at least three strips to make one continuous length of binding 65" (165cm) long, to be used for both book pages.

48 Join the binding strips on the diagonal and then press the length of binding fabric in half lengthways. For more detailed instructions and extra tips on quilt binding, see the 'Patchwork and Quilting' section at the beginning of the book.

49 Attach the binding to the inside left page starting at the base. Be careful that the ribbon ends are pinned or tucked away from the binding seams. Ensure the raw edges of the binding line up with the raw edges of the fabric. Sew in place with a ¼" (6mm) seam allowance. Be careful to

mitre the corners neatly, and join the binding ends neatly also. This step is a little fiddly because of the short length of the base of the stitchy book page.

50 When finished, fold the binding over towards the front cover and pin or clip in place. Using a single strand of polyester bobbin thread, blind stitch the binding to the front of the cover with small, fine stitches. For more detail about blind stitching, see the 'Stitch Library'.

51 Repeat the same process to sew the remaining binding onto the front of the inside right page. Then fold the binding over towards the back cover and blind stitch in place.

52 Place the bound front cover piece over the right hand page piece and pin or clip together along the left hand straight edge.

53 Using a double strand of neutral coloured sewing thread, whip stitch the binding together along the left hand straight edge, from the base to approximately 4" (10cm) up the left hand side. This will join both stitchy book pages together.

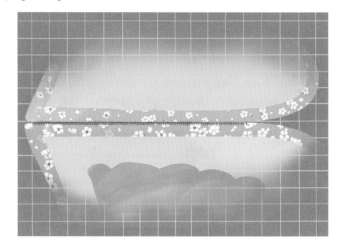

(whip stitch on binding)

54 Fill your stitchy book with pins, needles and cards of floss. Pop a small pair of scissors into the centre loop of the pink felt and lace strip on the top left hand page. Thread the ribbon through the scissor handles and tie a bow to secure them in place. Fold the stitchy book closed and tie a bow with the side ribbons. Your sewing kit is all prepped and ready for stitching on the go!

TIP: Customise the stitchy kit by adding extra pockets and c

Busy Bee Pincushion

When you're busy making and creating
something special in your sewing space, you
need a pincushion that will be large enough to hold
all sorts of pins and needles and won't get lost amongst
your fabrics and trims. It has to be beautiful too! The Busy
Bee pincushion is full of gorgeous little details that make
this so much more than a practical piece. Pair it with the
matching Honey Hive Stitchy Book.

Finished Size
Approximately 5 ½" (14 cm) square and
2 ¼" (5.7 cm) high

Materials

✓ Three 2" (5cm) squares of floral fabric for hexagon flower petals

✓ Three 2" (5cm) squares of floral fabric for alternating hexagon petals

✓ One 2" (5cm) square of print fabric for hexagon flower centre

✓ One 1 ½" (4cm) square of print fabric for the ¾" hexie detail

✓ 7 ½" (19cm) square of print fabric for pincushion base

✓ 7 ½" (19cm) square of natural coloured linen for pincushion top

✓ Paper backed fusible appliqué bonding web like Vliesofix

✓ Scraps of wool felt in two shades of green for the leaves

✓ Scraps of wool felt in white and two shades of pink for the flowers

✓ Scraps of wool felt in white, beige and pale pink for the bee

✓ DMC floss in 3713 (very light salmon), 452 (mid shell grey), Ecru, white (B5200)

✓ Water erasable pen

✓ Busy Bee Pincushion template

✓ Thick paper to create hexagon shapes

✓ Glue basting pen

✓ 60 weight polyester bobbin thread in white, grey or beige

✓ Milliner's needle in size 9

✓ Two ⅝" (1.5cm) diameter decorative buttons

✓ 4" (10cm) long-shank doll needle (ensure eye fits through decorative buttons)

✓ Polyester hobby fill

✓ Freezer paper

✓ Press cloth or cotton fabric scrap

✓ Rotary cutter, ruler and mat

✓ General sewing supplies

INSTRUCTIONS

TIP: For help with the different stitch types used in this project, please see the Stitch Library.

1 Use the template provided to trace and cut seven ¾" hexagon shapes from heavy paper.

2 Glue baste seven hexagons onto the paper shapes, using the 2" (5cm) squares of floral fabric. Make three hexagons from one floral print and three from another. These will form the flower petals. Make the last hexagon from the third fabric to form the centre of the flower. For more detailed instructions on making and joining hexagons, see the English Paper Piecing Techniques section at the beginning of the book.

TIP: I 'fussy cut' the fabric so that there is a flower or bee featured on each hexagon.

3 Arrange the hexagons into the flower shape, alternating the floral petals.

4 Whip stitch the sides together using 60 weight bobbin thread and a milliner's needle.

5 Remove the papers and press.

6 Trace around the outside of the hexagon flower shape onto the paper side of the fusible appliqué bonding web. Cut out the flower shape about ⅛" (3mm) in from the drawn line. Follow the manufacturer's instructions and use a warm iron to secure the bonding web to the wrong side of the hexagon flower. Peel off the backing paper.

7 Fold the 7 ½" (19cm) square of linen in half, then half again, and finger press the point, to find the centre of the panel. Open out.

8 Position the hexagon flower in the centre of the right side of the panel (over the centre fold). Press the flower in place with a warm iron, then secure the edges of the flower using a blind stitch. Use a single strand of bobbin thread and milliner's needle.

9 Use a clear acrylic ruler and a water erasable marker to draw quilting lines around the outside edge of the hexagon flower and on the inside edge of the centre hexagon, around ⅛" (3mm) in from the edge.

legs with two strands of the same floss. Use six strands of the grey floss to sew five straight lines across the abdomen to mark the bee's stripes. Highlight the wings with running stitch in two strands of white floss. When the stitching is complete, remove all drawn lines using a damp cloth.

15 Place the square of pincushion base fabric over the linen square with right sides facing. Using a ¼" (6mm) seam allowance, sew all four sides together leaving a 3 ½" (9cm) gap on the side opposite the bee appliqué and embroidery. This space will form the turning gap for the pincushion.

16 Using a clear acrylic ruler, measure ¾" (2cm) in from the seam lines in each corner and mark those corners with a square.

17 Use scissors to carefully cut out each corner.

18 Pinch the corners together so the side seams meet in the middle. Finger press the seams open and then stitch down the seam, again using a ¼" (6mm) seam allowance.

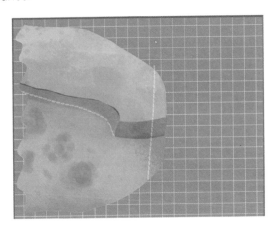

10 Use three strands of very light salmon floss to quilt around the outside of the hexagon flower using a fine running stitch. Stitch the inside of the centre hexagon with three strands of Ecru floss. Use a damp cloth to remove the quilting lines then press the panel once dry.

11 Trace the bee shapes onto fusible webbing and roughly cut around each one. Use a press cloth to protect the felt and iron the webbing onto the felt. Use white felt for the wings, beige for the body and pale pink for the abdomen.

12 Cut out each shape on the drawn template line and peel off the backing paper. Using the template as a guide, position the bee shapes underneath the right hand side of the base of the hexagon flower. Be sure it is positioned at least 1 ½" (4cm) from the bottom right corner. Secure in place with a warm iron.

19 Repeat this process to 'box' all four corners.

20 Turn the pincushion the right way out through the turning gap.

21 Fold the sides of the turning gap over ¼" (6mm) to match the seam allowance and finger press them.

22 Firmly fill the pincushion with small handfuls of polyester hobby fill. Be sure to firmly press the fill into each of the boxed corners too.

TIP: Here's an extra tip. Before adding hobby fill, place a 4 ½" (11.5cm) pouch stuffed with rice (or a similar product) to the inside base of the pincushion, to help weigh the pincushion down.

13 Use a water erasable pen to trace the curved bee flight line. Be sure it lines up under the bee's abdomen. Embroider the line using two strands of very light salmon floss and running stitch.

14 Appliqué the raw edges of the felt bee. Whip stitch the bee body with small, fine stitches using a single strand of mid shell grey floss. Back stitch the antenna and

23 Pin the turning gap opening in the pincushion closed (using the finger pressed seam folds as a guide). Using a single strand of bobbin thread, blind stitch the pincushion closed.

24 Trace the ¾" hexagon onto thick paper and cut out. Glue baste the 1 ½" (4cm) square of print quilter's cotton onto the paper and then remove the paper.

25 Pin the ½" hexagon onto the side on the right of the bee appliqué. Position it towards the right hand corner, making sure it has a flat side on the top and bottom and the points line up with the side seam in the pincushion. Use a single strand of bobbin thread to blind stitch the hexagon in place.

26 Using three strands of Ecru floss, quilt around the top of the pincushion about ⅛" (3mm) above the side seams, and over the top of the small hexagon detail. Hide the beginning and end of your stitching behind the hexagon.

27 Use the water erasable pen to mark the centre point on the top of the hexagon flower and the centre of the base.

28 Thread your doll needle with a long length of 6 stranded Ecru floss. Knot one end with a double knot and trim the excess. Bring the needle up through the base of the pincushion and through the centre mark in the middle hexagon on the top.

29 Bring the needle back down through the top of the pincushion and out through the base (just beside the marked centre point). Pull firmly to gently pinch the centre of the pincushion down.

30 Thread the button (for the pincushion base) onto the floss and sew in place, heading back up through the centre hole in the top.

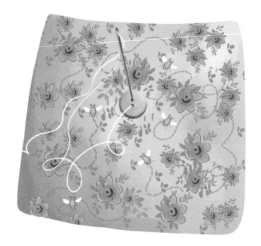

31 Position the top button in place. Secure both buttons by sewing through them a few times.

32 When the buttons are secure, bring the needle out through the base of the pincushion under the button but near the button stitching. Wind the floss around the bottom button a few times.

33 Enter the needle into the pincushion again and bring it out one side seam. Trim the extra floss length.

34 Make three felt flowers and three leaves to adorn the pincushion top. Trace the leaf and flower petal shapes (from the template) onto freezer paper and roughly cut out.

35 Iron the leaf shape onto the pale green felt and cut out on the line. Reuse the template to cut out a second pale green leaf and one darker green leaf. For more tips on using freezer paper see the 'Working With Felt' section.

36 Iron the flower petal shape to the flower felt. Reuse the template to cut out five petal shapes for each of the three flowers, in white, pale pink and darker pink.

37 Line up the five flower petals for each flower in a straight line. Using a sewing thread colour to match the flower felt, sew a small running stitch across the straight base of each petal in the row (using one continuous length of thread). When beginning and ending the stitching, ensure that the needle enters and exits the felt on the same side of each petal.

38 Gather the felt by pulling the thread firmly then manipulate the gathers. When you're happy with the flower shape, sew some small stitches through the back of the felt to secure the flower and ensure that it keeps its shape. The petals will overlap each other. Repeat this process to sew three flowers; white, pale pink and darker pink. Change thread colours to match each flower.

39 Pin the flowers and leaves onto the top of the pincushion until you are happy with the arrangement. Position them on the corner opposite to the appliqué bee.

40 Thread your needle with green thread to match the leaf felt. Fold the leaf in half and sew a small stitch around the fold.

41 With the thread still intact, attach the leaves to the pincushion with small, neat stitches.

42 Using thread to match the felt flowers, sew each flower in place by disguising the stitches between the overlapping petals and folds.

43 Add some pretty sewing pins because your lovely pincushion is all ready for use!

Polly Plaits Hoop Art

You can count on the smile from
Polly Plaits to warm both your heart and
your home. Polly's pretty plaits certainly stand out,
but it's her flower crown that really makes a statement.
Using appliqué and hand embroidery, this embroidery hoop
wall art project is a great introduction to working with felt.
You'll even learn how to ensure the back of the hoop looks
as pretty as the front. Being completely hand stitched, this
is the perfect project for sewing on the go.

Finished Size
8" (20.5cm) across

Materials

- ✓ 11" (28cm) square of floral fabric
- ✓ 11" (28cm) square of fusible interfacing
- ✓ 8" (20.5cm) timber embroidery hoop
- ✓ 7 ¾" (20cm) circle of wool felt for hoop backing
- ✓ 5" (12.5cm) square of cream wool felt for the face
- ✓ 5" (12.5cm) x 3" (7.5cm) pink wool felt for the hair
- ✓ 3" (7.5cm) x 12" (30.5cm) pink wool felt for the plaits
- ✓ Five 3" (8cm) x ¾" (2cm) wool felt scraps for flowers (to match background fabric – e.g. peach, lemon, pink, blue, pale blue)
- ✓ Two 1" (2.5cm) x 1 ½" (4cm) wool felt scraps in different shades of green for leaves
- ✓ DMC floss in Ecru, 3716 (very light dusty rose), 3790 (ultra dark beige grey)
- ✓ Embroidery needle
- ✓ Sewing needle and general sewing thread to match felt flower colours
- ✓ Paper backed fusible appliqué bonding web like Vliesofix
- ✓ Freezer paper
- ✓ Thin tissue paper
- ✓ 4 quilting clips or laundry pegs to hold plaits together
- ✓ 16" (40.5cm) of ⅜" (1cm) wide ribbon for plait bows
- ✓ Water erasable marker
- ✓ Pink colour pencil
- ✓ Polly Plaits template
- ✓ General sewing supplies

TIP: Before you begin sewing, see the Working With Felt section for helpful tips and tricks.

INSTRUCTIONS

1 Iron the fusible interfacing to the wrong side of the fabric square (by following the manufacturer's instructions).

2 Trace the Polly Plaits hair and face template onto fusible appliqué webbing and roughly cut out. For more tips on the process of appliqué, see the Appliqué Techniques section.

3 Iron the fusible webbing to the wool felt. Use the cream felt square for the face and smaller pink piece for the hair. Carefully cut out each shape on the template line and then peel off the backing paper.

4 Position the cream felt face in the centre of the fabric square (with the fusible webbing facing the fabric). Secure the felt to the fabric with a warm iron.

5 Using a water erasable pen, mark the face at the point where the hair meets the sides of the face (as indicated by a dot on the template).

6 Use two strands of Ecru DMC floss to blanket stitch the base of the face from one dot, down and along the bottom of the face to the other dot. You won't need to stitch around the top, as it will be covered by the pink hair.

7 Make two plaits to attach to the face. Cut 3" (8cm) x 12" (30.5cm) pink wool felt into six strips, each measuring ½" (12mm) wide and 12" (30.5cm) long.

8 Lay three felt strips over the top of one another, and sew them together with a few small stitches at the top. Use a quilting clip or peg to securely hold the top while you loosely plait the felt, leaving about 2" (5cm) at the end. Use a peg or quilting clip to hold the ends in place, while you secure them with a few small stitches again. Remove the clips / pegs. Trim the bottom so that the ends are a similar shape and the plaits are the same length.

9 Repeat this process with the other three strips of felt, to create the second plait.

10 Position the plaits on Polly's head, over the dots marked with the water erasable marker.

11 Position the piece of pink felt hair over the top half of Polly's face. Be sure that you catch the top of the plaits under this felt. At this stage you may wish to baste stitch the plaits in place. See more about baste stitching in the Stitch Library.

12 Iron the felt hair piece to fuse it in place. Use a small running stitch to appliqué the hair piece and plaits to the face. Use three strands of dusty rose DMC floss.

13 Finish Polly's plaits by tying a bow around the base of each plait. Trim the bow ends and heat seal to prevent fraying.

14 Sew the face details onto Polly. To do this, trace the face template shape and eye and mouth details onto thin tissue paper and cut out. Pin the tissue paper over the felt face. Ensure that the plaits do not cover the facial details.

15 Using three strands of DMC floss, back stitch the facial details, straight through the tissue paper. Use the beige grey for the eyes and dusty rose for the mouth.

16 When you've finished stitching, hold the stitches with one hand as you gently tear away the paper with the other. Tease any stray pieces of paper out from under the stitches with your needle (if necessary).

17 Tint Polly's cheeks by softly drawing circle shapes with pink colour pencil on either side of her mouth.

18 Make the flowers for Polly's crown. Trace the flower and leaf pattern from the Polly Plaits template onto freezer paper, and roughly cut out. Iron the freezer paper onto the flower felt, cut out the scalloped felt shape and peel off the freezer paper. Repeat this process to cut out flowers in five different colours. Use the same process to trace and cut two leaves in light green and two leaves in medium green.

19 Using a sewing thread colour to match the felt, sew a small running stitch across the straight base of the flower. When beginning and ending the stitching, ensure that the needle enters and exits the felt on the same side. Gather the felt by pulling the thread firmly then manipulate the gathers. When you're happy with the flower shape, sew some small stitches through the back of the felt to secure the flower and ensure that it keeps its shape. Repeat this process to sew five flowers.

20 Arrange the flowers across the top of Polly's head, including two leaves on the top and two under the crown. Sew the flowers in place using sewing thread to match your felt. Ensure your stitches cannot be seen from the front of the felt.

21 Place the appliqué into the embroidery hoop and centre the design, ensuring the screw is positioned at the top. Tighten the screw, pulling the fabric taut as you go.

22 Trim the fabric approximately 1" (2.5cm) from the outside edge of the hoop.

23 Thread your needle with a long single length of sewing thread. Starting at the top of the hoop, stitch a loose running stitch (about ½" (13mm) from the fabric edge), all the way around the outside edge.

24 When the stitching meets at the top, gather the thread to draw the fabric in. Secure the thread with a few stitches.

25 Finish the hoop, by securing a 7 ¾" (20cm) circle of felt to the back. Centre the felt over the hoop and whip stitch in place with evenly spaced stitches. (The Stitch Library has more detail on the different stitch types used in this project.)

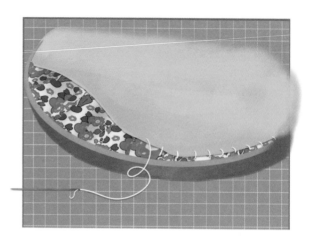

26 Hang Polly on the wall using the screw closure on the centre top of the hoop. Add extra ribbon to the screw to make a hanging loop if required.

Flower Friends Quilt

Who could resist the smiles from the darling flower friends on this pram quilt? The white background provides the perfect backdrop for the beautiful florals and pretty patterns found in the fabric prints used for this design. Showcase an entire fabric range as I have done, by using different prints for the flowers, the square details, the scrappy binding and even the simple patchwork back. The Flower Friends Quilt brings together a range of techniques including embroidery, appliqué, patchwork and quilting. It's perfectly sized for a cosy lap quilt or a baby's bassinet too.

Finished Size
Approximately 27 ½" (70 cm)
wide and 31 ½" (80 cm) high

FABRIC SELECTION

This quilt uses fat quarters from 17 different prints in a single fabric collection. However, it would look just as lovely using three or more pretty florals on a simple plain background. So you could choose a treasured fabric bundle or show off just a few prints from your favourite range.

FOR THE QUILT TOP

✓ Eighteen 2 ½" (6.4cm) squares of floral print fabric (I used 9 prints, cutting two from each print) for the inner border

✓ Twenty-one 2 ½" (6.4cm) squares of white fabric (18 for the inner border, 3 for the flower face appliqué)

✓ 14 ½" (36.8cm) x 18 ½" (47cm) of white fabric for the centre panel

✓ 5" (12.7cm) x 22 ½" (57.2cm) of white fabric for the left and right outer border

✓ 5" (12.7cm) x 27 ½" (69.9cm) of white fabric for the top and bottom outer border

✓ Three 5" (12.7cm) squares of floral print fabric for the flower appliqué

✓ Three 2 ½" (6.4cm) x 1 ½" (3.8cm) pieces of three different plain coloured fabric for the flower hair appliqué (I used pink, apricot and blue)

✓ 8" (20cm) x 3" (7.6cm) of green fabric for the leaf appliqué

✓ Paper backed fusible appliqué bonding web like Vliesofix

✓ DMC floss in 603 (cranberry) and 3790 (ultra dark beige grey)

✓ Embroidery needle

✓ Water or heat erasable marking pen

FOR THE QUILT BACK

✓ Six 19" (48cm) x 6" (15cm) rectangles of mixed fabrics

✓ Six 10" (25.5cm) x 6" (15cm) rectangles of mixed fabrics

TO FINISH THE QUILT

✓ 28" (71cm) x 32" (81.3cm) of quilt wadding

✓ Fourteen 7 ½" (19cm) x 2 ½" (6.5cm) strips of fabric for the binding

✓ Two 14" (35.6cm) x 2 ½" (6.5cm) strips of print for the tails or ends of the binding

✓ 60 weight polyester bobbin thread in white, grey or beige

✓ Milliner's needle in size 9

OTHER NOTIONS AND SUPPLIES

✓ Rotary cutter, ruler and mat

✓ Quilt basting (adhesive) spray

✓ Quilting clips

✓ General sewing supplies including sewing machine, iron and ironing board.

INSTRUCTIONS

NOTE: All seam allowances for this project are ¼" (6mm).

Pre-cut all fabrics from the materials list using a rotary cutter, self-healing mat and ruler (for accuracy).

TIP: This project is best stitched with a walking foot when quilting on your sewing machine. A ¼" foot is great for accuracy when piecing. Change to a clear-based appliqué foot when stitching the flowers.

MAKE THE QUILT TOP

SEW THE BORDER ROWS

1 Arrange the 18 print and 18 plain white fabric squares into four rows with nine squares in each row. Two rows will begin and end with the print squares (and will form the top and bottom of the block). The remaining two rows will begin and end with plain white squares (and will form the left and right sides of the block). When you are happy with the placement of the squares take a photograph of the layout (so you can refer back to it as you sew).

2 Sew each row together. Place the first two squares (print and plain from the top row) together with right sides facing and sew along one side. Select the next print square in the sequence and with right sides facing sew it to the opposite side of the plain square. Continue with all squares in the row.

3 When the row is complete, use a hot iron to press all the seams toward the print side (so they do not show behind the plain white cotton).

4 Continue alternating between print and plain squares to complete all four rows of nine squares. Press.

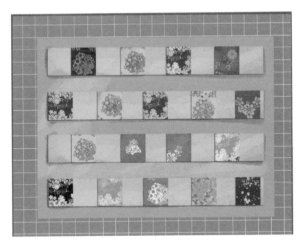

5 With right sides facing, pin the left and right rows to the left and right of the plain white centre panel. Stitch in place and press away from the centre panel.

6 With right sides facing, pin the top and bottom rows to the top and bottom of the plain white centre panel. Ensure the seams meet up neatly at the corner of each panel. Stitch in place and press seams away from the centre panel.

The panel should measure 18.5" (47cm) wide and 22.5" (57.2cm) tall.

7 With right sides facing, pin the left and right plain outer border pieces to the left and right of the centre panel.

8 Stitch in place and press seams away from the centre panel.

9 With right sides facing, pin and sew the top and bottom plain outer border pieces to the top and bottom of the centre panel. Press the seams away from the centre panel.

The completed quilt top panel should measure 27.5" wide and 31.5" tall.

APPLIQUÉ THE QUILT

For more information about the appliqué process, please see the Appliqué Techniques section.

10 Trace the appliqué shapes onto the paper side of the fusible appliqué bonding web. You will need;
• 2 large flowers
• 2 large faces
• 2 large hair
• 4 large leaves
• 1 small flower
• 1 small face
• 1 small hair
• 1 small leaf

11 Roughly cut around each piece and iron it to the wrong side of your chosen fabrics for each appliqué design.

•2 large and 1 small face shape onto the white cotton
•2 large and 1 small hair shape onto the 3 plain coloured pieces
•2 large and 1 small flower shape onto the 3 print squares
•4 large and 1 small leaf shape onto the plain green strip

12 Cut out the designs on the line and peel off the backing paper, ready to arrange on the quilt top.

13 Play around with the placement until you are happy with the layout. For example, arrange the flower petals at angles to create more interest. Place the ends of two large leaves under each large flower and one small leaf end under the small flower. Then use a warm iron to secure the designs in place.

14 Appliqué around the raw edges of each of these leaf then flower shapes using a small blanket stitch on your sewing machine. Alternatively, you may wish to use a straight or zig zag stitch on your machine, or sew the appliqués by hand. Use sewing thread to complement the colours of your fabrics.

15 Centre the faces on the flower shapes. Overlap the hair on the top of the faces. Place the hair at a slight angle for interest. Press in place.

16 Appliqué around the raw edge of the base of each face shape using white thread. Then change thread colour to blanket stitch around the outside edges of the three different hair shapes.

17 Using the template as a guide, trace or transfer the three face designs to the white flower faces. Ensure you use the large face for the large flowers and small face for the small flower.

18 Using three strands of DMC floss and an embroidery needle, back stitch the designs using beige gray for the eyes and cranberry for the mouths. See the Stitch Library for more detailed instructions for back stitch.

When the embroidery is complete, remove the water erasable marker lines using a damp cloth.

19 Carefully press the completed quilt top and set aside.

MAKE THE QUILT BACK

20 Take the quilt backing fabric rectangles and arrange them to form six rows of one short and one long rectangle, alternating rectangle lengths in each row. When you are happy with the fabric placement, take a photograph that you can refer to during sewing.

21 Create six rows by sewing the side seams of the rectangles together in each row. Pin the rectangles right sides together along the short edge and sew with a ¼" (6mm) seam allowance. Press the seams open.

22 Sew the six rows together using the same method and again press the seams open. Press the quilt back well. It is larger than the quilt top so it can accommodate the quilting process.

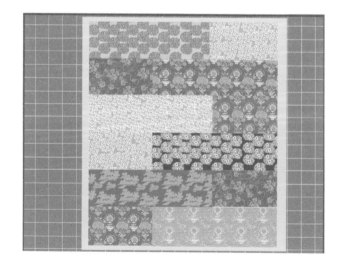

ASSEMBLE THE QUILT

23 Place the quilt wadding on a flat surface. Following the manufacturer's instructions, spray the wrong side of the pressed quilt top with a coating of quilt basting spray. Centre the quilt top over the wadding and gently press in place with your hands, being sure to smooth out any air pockets, lumps or wrinkles with your hands.

24 Using the same method as before, spray the wrong side of the pressed quilt backing with a coating of quilt basting spray. Place the quilt backing right side down on a flat surface. Position the right side of the quilt top and wadding over the centre of the quilt backing and gently press in place with your hands. Ensure that the seams for each row on the backing run straight when positioned behind the quilt top. Your 'quilt sandwich' is now assembled.

25 Quilt the 'quilt sandwich' with your desired quilting method. This quilt was professionally quilted to showcase and highlight the little details in the quilt. However, you may wish to do your own quilting on your home machine or even hand quilt it. You can read more about quilting in the 'Patchwork and Quilting Techniques' section.

26 After the quilting process is complete, trim down the quilt so that it is ready for binding. It's important to use a rotary cutter, mat and ruler to square up the quilt and to make sure the left and right sides are at right angles to the top and bottom of the quilt. After trimming, you may also wish to sew a scant 1/8" (3mm) seam around the outside edge to help keep the quilt sandwich together for binding.

BIND THE QUILT

27 The patchwork binding on this quilt helps showcase even more pretty floral prints. I used eight different prints to cut the sixteen required strips for binding.

Create one continuous length of binding fabric by joining the fourteen 7 ½" (19cm) x 2 ½" (6.5cm) strips. Place them right sides together and sew a straight seam across the short 2 ½" sides. Then add a 14" (35.6cm) x 2 ½" (6.5cm) strip to each end. The extra length in these strips create tails for joining the binding at the base of the quilt. For more detailed instructions and extra tips on quilt binding, see the Quilt Binding section at the beginning of the book.

28 Once all sixteen strips are joined, press all the seams open. Then fold the fabric strip in half lengthways and press. Find the centre point of the binding (the seam between the 8th and 9th fabric pieces). Position this seam over the centre top of the quilt. Pin or clip the binding to the front of the quilt ensuring the raw edges of the binding line up with the raw edges of the quilt. The long tails will meet at the centre on the base of the quilt.

29 Being careful to leave enough binding tail to join together, sew the binding in place with a ¼" (6mm) seam allowance. Mitre the corners neatly.

30 When joining the binding on the base, use a straight seam (to match the others) instead of the traditional diagonal seam. Find the centre of the bottom of the quilt and mark with a pin. Open the binding fabrics and pin them right sides together so that they meet over this centre line in the quilt. Mark the line with an erasable pen if you wish.

31 Sew a straight seam and fold the binding in half to ensure it fits neatly across the base of the quilt (without any puckers). Trim the extra length off the binding tails

32 Finger press the seam open and then fold the binding in half again. Continue to sew the binding down on the base of the quilt.

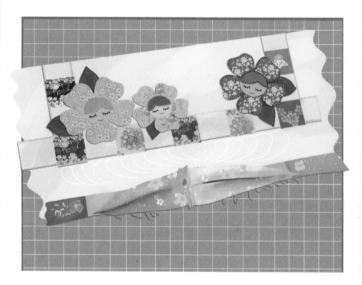

33 When finished, fold, then press the binding over towards the back of the quilt. Using a single strand of 60 weight bobbin thread and the milliner's needle, blind stitch the binding to the back of the quilt with small, fine stitches. For more about blind stitching, see the Stitch Library.

Lullaby Kitty Felt Doll

*The playful Lullaby Kitty
is a cheeky little cat. Completely hand-stitched with wool
felt, she's perfect for gentle play by older children. Lullaby
Kitty loves her naptime too. She comes with instructions to
machine sew a dainty nightgown. You can then make her a Sweet
Dreams Sleeping Bag; the perfect accessory to
pop her in at rest times!*

Finished Size
Approximately 7 ½" (19cm) tall (including the
ears) and 5" (12.5cm) wide (from one hand to
the other)

55

Materials

FOR THE KITTY;

✔ 8" (20.5cm) x 11 ½" (29cm) cream wool felt for the kitty body

✔ Pale Pink wool felt scraps for inner ears, cheeks and tummy

✔ Beige wool felt scraps for head patch and nose

✔ DMC floss; 948 (very light peach), 3864 (light mocha beige), 3790 (ultra dark beige gray), 3713 (very light salmon)

✔ Embroidery needle

✔ Polyester hobby fill

✔ Stuffing tool (or similar item like a chopstick)

✔ Water erasable marker

✔ Freezer paper

✔ Tissue paper

✔ Lullaby Kitty template

FOR THE LULLABY NIGHTGOWN;

✔ Two 5" (13cm) wide x 4 ½" (11.5cm) high rectangles of fabric

✔ Two 8" (20cm) lengths of 1/8" (3mm) wide pale pink grosgrain ribbon (with heat sealed ends to prevent fraying)

✔ 10" (25.5cm) of cotton crochet lace ⅜" (1cm) wide

✔ Small decorative button

✔ Bodkin or narrow safety pin to thread ribbon

✔ Sewing machine and general sewing notions

NOTES: The kitty is sewn with a blanket stitch, but a whip stitch can also be used. This may be quicker and easier for less experienced stitchers. Remember to refer to the Stitch Library and Working With Felt sections at the beginning of the book for help with stitch types, using freezer paper, and transferring embroidery details to felt.

Use two strands of DMC floss for all stitching in this pattern.

Knot the end of the floss to begin stitching. Be sure that any stitching is started on the wrong side of the felt, so that the knots are not visible on the finished work.

Secure all completed stitching with a few small back stitches on the wrong side (or inside) of the felt.

INSTRUCTIONS FOR THE LULLABY KITTY

1 Trace the Lullaby Kitty template pieces onto freezer paper and roughly cut around the outside of each shape. The freezer paper templates are reusable.

2 Iron the freezer paper templates to the wool felt with a warm iron. Cut out the required felt shapes using felt cutting scissors and peel off the freezer paper. You will need the following pieces.

Cream felt;
• Two head pieces
• Two body pieces
• Four ear pieces
• Four arm pieces
• Four leg pieces
• One tail piece

Pink felt;
• Two inner ear pieces
• Two cheek circles
• One tummy piece

Beige felt;
• One head patch piece
• One nose piece

3 Sew the Ears. Divide the four ear pieces into two pairs that are mirror images (so that you have a left ear and a right ear). Position the pink inner ear shapes over the top ear pieces of each pair. Sew the pink inner ear piece to the top ear piece of each pair by sewing a very fine, small running stitch along the outside curved edge with peach DMC floss. Don't stitch the straight base of the ear. We'll do that later.

Now sew the two ear pieces of one pair together with a small blanket stitch, using very light salmon DMC floss. Start at the base of one side of the ear and sew up and around the point and back down to the base of the other side. Keep the floss intact. Stuff the ear firmly with a small amount of hobby fill. Then sew the gap closed using a fine whip stitch. The base of the ear will be hidden between the two felt layers of the head. Secure the floss well at the end. Repeat this process to sew the second ear, making sure it is a mirror image of your first ear. Pop the ears aside.

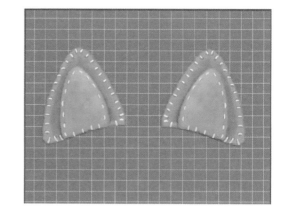

4 Sew the Legs. Divide the four leg pieces into two pairs that are mirror images of each other. Sew each leg together using very light salmon DMC floss and a small, fine blanket stitch. Start at the top of the leg and stitch down and around the base of the leg and back up to the top. Stop stitching about ½" (12mm) from the top but leave the floss intact. Stuff the leg through the opening using hobby fill. A stuffing tool or a chopstick can help you manoeuvre stuffing into hard to reach places. Only add tiny amounts of stuffing at a time.

5 When the leg is firmly stuffed, continue to blanket stitch the side of the leg up to the top. Then close the top of the leg (along the straight edge) with a fine whip stitch. Repeat this process to sew the second leg. Pop these aside.

6 Sew the Arms. Divide the four arm pieces into two pairs that are mirror images of each other. Use the same method as described for the legs (step 4) to sew a left and right arm. Pop the arms aside.

7 Embroider the Kitty's face details. Trace the face onto tissue or tracing paper and cut out. Pin the tracing paper over one piece of felt face. Back stitch through the tracing paper to embroider the eyes and mouth details with ultra dark beige gray embroidery floss. Remove the tracing paper when the stitching is complete by gently tearing it away.

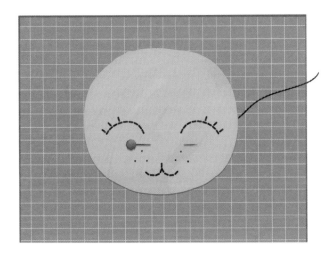

Use the template and the mouth embroidery as a guide to position the kitty's nose. Using light mocha beige DMC floss, secure the nose in place with a small, fine blanket stitch or running stitch. You will need to hold the nose as you stitch.

Position the beige head patch on the centre top of kitty's head and pin in place. Use light mocha beige DMC floss and a fine running stitch to secure the head patch. Start at the top of the head, stitch down to the point and up the other side. Do not stitch along the top of the head though. This will be completed when the whole kitty is assembled. Consult the template to determine where to stitch the two

pink cheek circles. Hold each cheek in place and then use very light peach DMC floss and a fine running stitch to secure them.

Use a water erasable marker (and the template as a guide) to mark three dots on each side of the kitty's nose. Using ultra dark beige gray DMC floss, stitch a French knot over each dot. The face is now complete.

8 Sew the kitty's tummy. Using the template as a guide, position the tummy piece over one of the body shapes and stitch in place using a fine running stitch and very light peach DMC floss.

9 Assemble the front and back of the kitty. Overlap the face piece over the tummy piece by about ¼" (6mm). Pin together and then blanket stitch the two pieces together. Secure the end of the stitching well. Assemble the back of the kitty body in the same way. Be sure the back will be the same size as the front and that they will match up when placed wrong sides together.

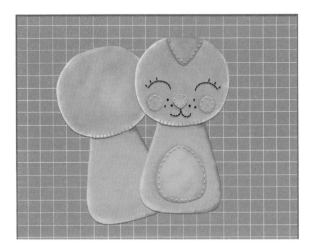

10 Sew the kitty together. This stage of the assembly is a little fiddly, but the results are worth it in the end! You may wish to baste stitch (with large removable stitches) the arms, legs and ears in place before blanket stitching the body together. However, I find it easier to add these as I sew.

Place the back of the kitty right side down on a flat surface. Place the front of the kitty over the top (right side facing out). Use very light salmon DMC floss to match the kitty felt colour. Sew a couple of whip stitches at the right hand side of the neck seam to hold the front and back pieces together. Place the arm between the front and back pieces (overlapping it about ¼" or 5mm) just below this stitch. Blanket stitch the body pieces together being sure to catch the end of the arm in the seam. Continue to blanket stitch down the side of the body and around to the base of the kitty. Insert the legs and stitch in place as you continue to sew the front and back together. Stitch up the other side of the kitty and add the second arm. When the neck seam is reached, sew a couple of firm whip stitches to reinforce the stitching. Keep the floss intact.

11 Firmly stuff the body with small handfuls of hobby fill through the opening in the neck. Again, use a stuffing tool or chopstick to manoeuvre the stuffing inside.

12 Sew the head together by continuing to blanket stitch around the head shape. Add the ears into the seams so that they line up with the outside edges of the head patch. Stop sewing after stitching the second ear in place but keep the floss intact.

13 Use the gap between the ear and neck to finish firmly stuffing the kitty with small balls of hobby fill. Then continue blanket stitching to the neck seam to sew the kitty closed.

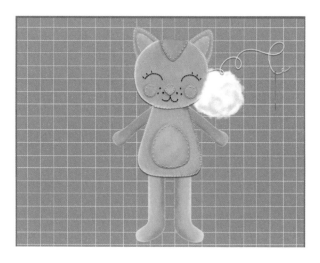

14 Sew the tail. Fold the tail in half lengthways. Starting at the narrowest end, whip stitch the edges of the felt piece together and pull the stitches firmly to make the tail slightly curl as you stitch. Stop sewing about ⅜" (1cm) before the end of the tail. Keep the floss intact.

15 Position the tail (over the bottom) on the back of the kitty so that it is pointing upwards. Flange the base of the felt tail out over the kitty's back. Using the same floss, stitch the tail in place by sewing through the back felt.

16 Now all kitty needs is a nightgown and bed! Sew the Lullaby Nightgown and Sweet Dreams Sleeping Bag for kitty too.

INSTRUCTIONS FOR THE LULLABY NIGHTGOWN

Lullaby Kitty's nightgown is a machine sewn pillowcase style sleeveless dress, with a casing at the neck for ribbon ties and a pretty lace trim at the hem.

1 Serge, Overlock or Zig Zag stitch around the outside edge of both fabric rectangles.

2 Place both rectangles together with right sides facing and the longest side 5" (13cm) at the bottom. Measure 2 ¼" (5.5cm) up from the base of the fabric and place a mark on the left and the right sides using the water erasable marker.

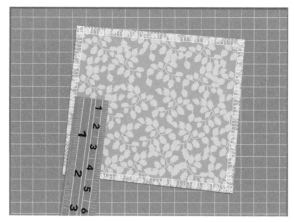

3 Sew one side of the fabric from the base to the mark, using a ¼" (6mm) seam allowance. Iron the seam open.

4 On the right side of the fabric, top stitch the open end of the seam with a very scant seam allowance. Stitch from the top of the fabric, down to the seam opening, stitch across two stitches and then back up the other side. This will form one arm opening.

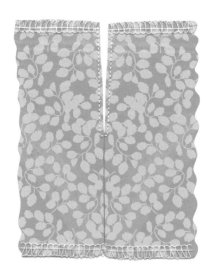

5 Add the lace trim to the base of the fabric. Place the lace strip over the fabric base with right sides facing, raw edges aligned. Stitch the lace in place with a straight stitch and a scant seam allowance (enough to cover the serging or overlocking edge).

6 Turn the lace down and press the seam allowance up towards the fabric.

7 Top stitch the seam with a scant seam allowance.

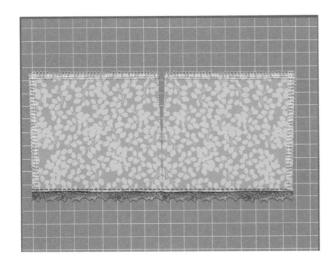

8 Fold the fabric in half with right sides together. Stitch the other side seam in the same way as the first side seam (from the fabric base up to the marker line). Iron the seam allowance open and repeat the previous process in step 4 to stitch the arm opening.

9 Ensure the dress is facing wrong side out. Fold down the open end of one side of the fabric by ¾" (2cm) and press. Repeat on the other side of the dress. Sew a straight stitch along the base of the fold on each side of the dress (over the overlocker / serger stitching). This will form a neck casing for the ribbon ties. Turn the dress right way out and press.

10 Use a bodkin or narrow safety pin to thread one 8" (20cm) length of ribbon through the front casing. Thread the other 8" (20cm) length of ribbon through the back casing.

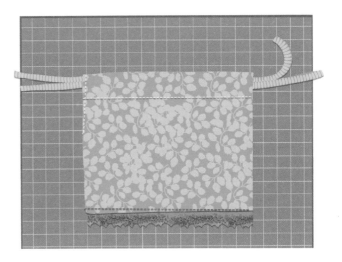

11 Pop the dress over the kitty with its arms through the openings on the side seams. Tie the ribbons in bows at either side of the kitty's neck.

12 Add a button or bow for a sweet decorative touch on the top stitching seam of the lace trim.

Kitty is all dressed and ready for bed!

Sweet Dreams Sleeping Bag

Made for Lullaby Kitty,
the Sweet Dreams Sleeping Bag is the perfect accessory
for our sleepy cat after a hard day of play. Featuring a front
panel of hand stitched elongated hexagons, this adorable
project is ideal for showcasing your favourite fabric prints.
Machine sewn, it will fit a doll or toy that measures 8"
(20cm) tall.

Finished Size
9 ¾" (25cm) high and 7 ¼" (18.5cm) wide

Materials

✓ *Twenty 2" (5cm) x 3" (7.5cm) rectangles of different floral fabrics (I had two pieces in each of 10 different fabrics)*

✓ *8" (20cm) x 10 ½" (26.5cm) of natural coloured linen for the top of the sleeping bag base*

✓ *8" (20cm) x 7" (17.5cm) of natural coloured linen to line the hexie top of the sleeping bag*

✓ *8" (20cm) x 10 ½" (26.5cm) of floral fabric for the backing of the sleeping bag base*

✓ *31" (79cm) Picot edge bias binding or double fold bias binding for outside of sleeping bag*

✓ *7 ¼" (18.5cm) Picot edge bias binding or double fold bias binding for top of sleeping bag pocket*

✓ *7 ¼" (18.5cm) cotton lace trim ⅜" (1cm) wide*

✓ *Two pieces of fusible fleece; 8" (20cm) x 7" (17.5cm) and 8" (20cm) x 10 ½" (26.5cm)*

✓ *Water erasable pen .*

✓ *Sweet Dreams Sleeping Bag template*

✓ *Thick paper to create twenty 1" elongated hexagon paper shapes*

✓ *Glue basting pen*

✓ *60 weight polyester bobbin thread in white, grey or beige*

✓ *Milliner's needle in size 9*

✓ *Leather Label or other trim for decorating the back of the sleeping bag (optional)*

✓ *Quilt basting (adhesive) spray*

✓ *General sewing supplies*

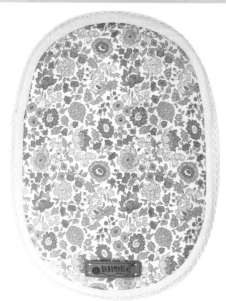

INSTRUCTIONS

NOTE: All seam allowances for this project are ¼" (6mm).

TIP: When machine sewing, this project is best stitched using a walking foot.

1 Use the template provided to trace and cut 20 identical 1" elongated hexagon paper shapes. Use each elongated hexagon paper to glue-baste 20 hexagons, each with different floral fabrics. For more detailed instructions on making and sewing elongated hexagons, see the English Paper Piecing Techniques at the beginning of the book.

2 Arrange the hexagons in a panel so that the flat sides are vertical and the points are facing the top and bottom. The rows will contain the following number of hexagons from top to bottom; Top row: 5, Second row: 6, Third row: 5, Bottom Row: 4

3 When you are happy with the layout, photograph your panel so that you can refer to the image as you stitch.

4 Hand sew the hexagon panel together using fine bobbin thread and a fine milliner's needle.

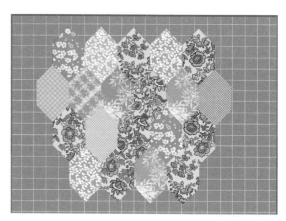

5 Remove the hexagon papers from the back of the panel, starting with those in the centre. Press the panel as you go, to help keep the hexagons in shape.

6 Use the 'Sleeping Bag Top' template to cut a lining from the small piece of fusible fleece or wadding. Follow the manufacturer's instructions to secure it to the back of the panel with a warm iron. Ensure that it is centred and that your hexagon seams are straight or square. It will fit snugly.

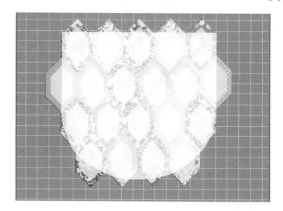

7 Cut the excess fabric away from around the fusible fleece. This will become the front of the sleeping bag top.

8 Spray the fusible fleece side of the hexagon panel with quilt basting spray and place the 8" (20cm) x 7" (17.5cm) piece of linen over the top. Press with your hands to fuse the two layers together and remove any wrinkles. Cut the linen to match the shape of the hexagon panel.

9 Pin the strip of lace (right side up) with its raw edge against the raw edge of the top of the hexagon panel. Stitch the lace in place using a scant ⅛" (3mm) seam allowance.

10 Continue to stitch around the outside edge of the whole hexagon piece (using the same scant seam allowance) to baste the floral fabric top, fleece and linen backing together.

11 Add the 7 ¼" (18.5cm) binding to the top edge of the panel over the lace. Open the double fold picot edge bias binding on one side. Line up the raw edge of the binding with its right side facing down along the raw edge of the top of the panel (over the lace). You may like to pin the binding in place. Stitch the binding in place along the first fold line.

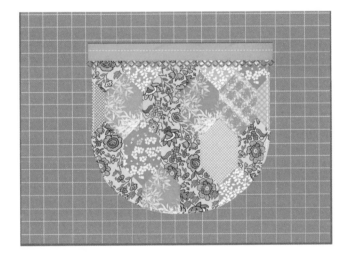

12 Fold the binding over so that the picot edge of the binding (or the centre fold of plain binding) is on the outside edge. Using a single strand of bobbin thread, blind stitch the bottom of the folded edge of the binding to the back of the pocket with small, fine stitches. See the Stitch Library for more information about blind stitching. The binding should reach over the raw fabric edges and cover over the machine stitched seam line sewn on the front. Set this piece aside.

13 Secure the large piece of fusible fleece to the sleeping bag backing fabric with a warm iron. Trace the Sleeping Bag template onto the fabric and cut out.

14 If you would like to add any embellishments to the back of the Sleeping Bag (like the handmade tag I stitched on the centre base), now is the time to add it.

15 Spray the fusible fleece side of the fabric with quilt basting spray and place the remaining piece of linen over the top. Press with your hands to fuse the two layers together and remove any wrinkles. Cut the linen to match the shape of the fabric and fleece panel.

16 Pin the top piece of the Sleeping Bag (with the elongated hexagons facing out) to the linen side of the back piece. If embellishments have been added to the back piece, ensure they are facing the correct way. Sew around the outside edge of the whole back piece, using a scant 1/8" (3mm) seam allowance. This will hold everything in place for binding.

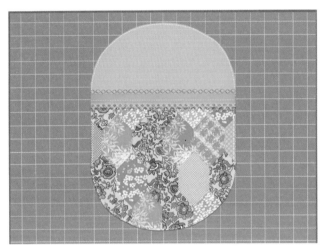

17 Bind the outside edge of the Sleeping Bag with the remaining binding. Open the binding and pin in place with right sides facing the Sleeping Bag. Fold the raw edge of the start of the binding over by ⅜" (1cm) and start sewing the binding where the pocket is attached on one side.

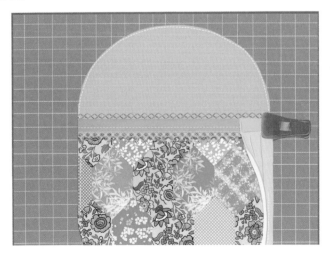

18 Continue to sew the binding around the outside edge of the Sleeping Bag on the binding's fold line. When you reach the starting point, overlap the folded edge of the binding by about 1" (2.5cm) and sew down on the same stitch line. Trim away any excess binding.

19 Fold the binding over towards the back of the quilt. Pin or clip in place. Blind stitch the binding to the back of the quilt in the same manner as before.

The Sleeping Bag is all ready for Lullaby Kitty! Make a tiny felt pillow or blanket for kitty too. Wouldn't that be sweet?

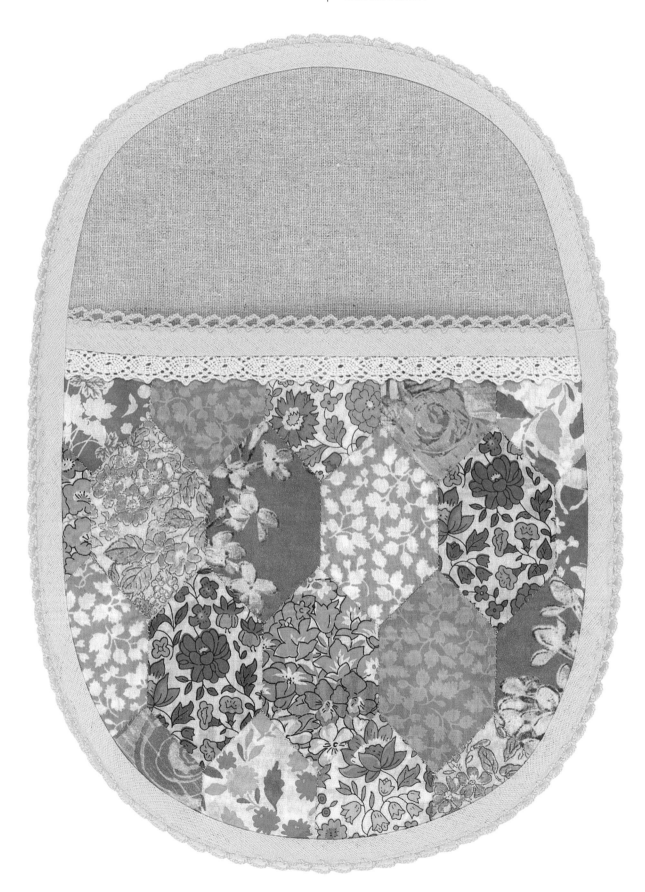

Tea Party Tea Towel

This delectable tea towel is almost too
pretty to use on the dishes! A quick and easy sew,
it includes four delicate hand appliqué designs to help
you practice your blanket stitching; a slice of cake, a tea
cup and saucer, a cupcake and a tea pot. It also includes
instructions to add a simple hanging loop.

Practical and pretty!

Finished Size
The finished tea towel is approximately 18" (46 cm)
across and 26" (66 cm) high. The appliqué panel is
18" (46 cm) across and 5" (12.5 cm) high.

Materials

✓ 20" (51cm) x 28" (71cm) fabric like linen or quilter's cotton for the tea towel

✓ 20" (51cm) x 6" (15cm) white cotton fabric for the appliqué panel

✓ Various fabric scraps in coordinating colours for the appliqué

✓ Paper backed fusible appliqué bonding web like Vliesofix

✓ 40" (102cm) white crochet lace trim (⅜" or 10mm wide)

✓ 6" (15cm) of white cotton twill tape (½" or 12mm wide)

✓ DMC floss - Ecru, 3326 (light rose), 601 (dark cranberry), 603 (cranberry)

✓ Embroidery needle

✓ Water or heat erasable marking pen

✓ Appliqué glue (optional)

✓ Tea party tea towel templates

INSTRUCTIONS

1 Trace the individual pattern pieces onto fusible webbing for appliqué. Where applicable, the templates have already been reversed. For more information, see the Appliqué Techniques section at the front of the book.

2 Roughly cut around each piece and iron to the wrong side of your chosen fabrics for each of the appliqué designs.

3 Cut out the designs on the lines and peel off the backing paper, ready to arrange on fabric.

4 Fold the short ends of the white cotton fabric panel over by one inch and press. This 1" space will become the seam allowance for the sides of the tea towel.

5 Arrange each of the appliqué designs on the white fabric panel in the following order; Cake Slice, Tea Cup, Cupcake, Tea Pot. Place the designs an equal distance apart and centred between the top and bottom edges of the panel. Ensure the cake slice and tea pot are no closer than ½" (12mm) from the 1" (2.5cm) seam allowance fold lines on the short ends.

Use the following guideline for fabric placement for each appliqué shape;

CAKE SLICE
• Place Side piece down first
• Add Side Strip to the centre of the Side
• Position Icing to over the top of the Side
• Overlap the Cream over the Icing and top of the Side

TEA CUP
• Position the Saucer first
• Place the Cup over the centre of the Saucer
• Slide the ends of the Handle under the side of the Cup
• Place the Mouth above the Cup but slide the bottom edge underneath so that the Cup is overlapping the Mouth
• Position the Band across the top of the Cup

CUPCAKE
• Place the Base down first
• Overlap the Top over the top edge of the Base
• Position the Icing to align with the curved edge of the Top

TEA POT
• Place the Pot down first
• Overlap the Lid over the top of the Pot
• Position the Handle and Spout on either side of the Pot, sliding the ends underneath
• Place the Band over the top of the Pot

When you are happy with the position of the four appliqués, use a warm iron to secure them in place.

6 Appliqué around the raw fabric edges of each of the shapes. You may choose to machine stitch with a straight, zig zag or blanket stitch. You may also wish to hand sew the appliqués with blanket stitch as I have done. For hand stitching, use two strands of DMC floss to stitch around each individual piece of fabric. See the Stitch Library for more tips on blanket stitch.

Use two strands of the following DMC floss colours for each design.

CAKE SLICE
• Cranberry for the cream, icing and side
• Ecru for the side strip

TEA CUP
• Cranberry for the cup and handle
• Light rose for the mouth and saucer
• Dark cranberry for the band

CUPCAKE
• Cranberry for the base
• Ecru for the top
• Light rose for the icing

TEA POT
• Light rose for the pot, spout and handle
• Cranberry for the lid
• Dark cranberry for the band

7 When the appliqué is complete, press the panel and then fold the top and bottom edges to the wrong side of the fabric by ½" (12mm).

8 Measure 6" (15cm) from the base of the tea towel fabric and rule a straight line across using a water or heat erasable marker. Cut the length of white lace trim in half. Lay one piece of the trim along the line so that the top edge just overlaps the line. Place the appliquéd fabric panel over the top edge of the lace trim and pin in place.

TIP: As an easy alternative, you may wish to use a very small amount of appliqué glue to help keep the lace and the panel in place. A quick press with the iron will dry the glue, eliminating the need for pins. This ensures your seam remains super straight. Also, the fabric and lace won't move around whilst sewing.

9 Top stitch the base of the panel and lace in place, sewing very close to the fabric edge.

10 Repeat the above steps to secure the top lace and sew the top edge of the panel. Simply measure a line on the tea towel fabric that is 5" above the base of the fabric panel. Ensure the lace and top of the panel sit nicely before pinning (or using the appliqué glue) and stitch in place.

11 To hem the tea towel, fold all the raw edges over ½" (12mm) towards the wrong side and press firmly.

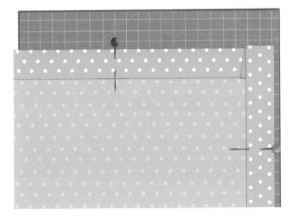

12 Use the following steps to mitre each corner. First, turn the folded corner over so that the outside edge of the fold line rests at the point where the two sides meet underneath.

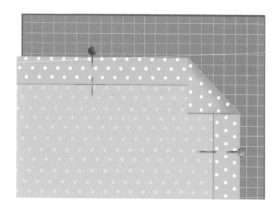

13 Trim this fold so that it lines up with the other folded edges.

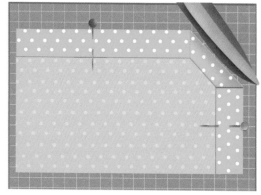

14 Fold all the sides over by another ½" (12mm) and press. Make sure that the folded edges meet in a diagonal at the centre of the corner.

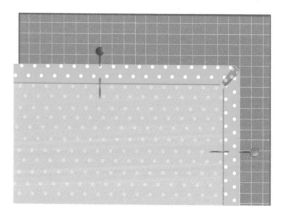

15 Repeat this process to mitre each corner. Pin all the sides and corners, ready for sewing.

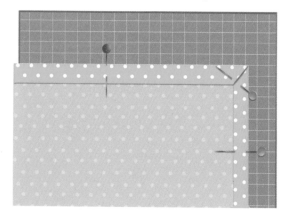

16 On the top left hand side of the tea towel, measure 3" (7.5cm) down from the top edge and make a small mark on the inside edge of the folded hem (with an erasable pen). Repeat this step to draw a mark 3" (7.5cm) from the left hand edge along the top also.

17 Position the twill tape so that it lines up across these lines. Trim the corners on the diagonal and tuck the twill tape under the folded hem. Pin in place.

18 Hem the tea towel, stitching very close to the fold line. Start the hem sewing at one side of the fabric panel. Stitch up along the folded edge to the corner, pivot your needle when it reaches the diagonal fold line in the mitre, and continue to stitch down to the next corner.

19 When the remaining sides are sewn and you reach the starting point, secure your stitching with a few small back stitches. Your tea towel is ready for use!

Pretty Petal Dilly Bag

This sweet and dainty drawstring bag is adorned
with petals that fan out beautifully when the pretty
ribbons are pulled. But it is practical too. Use it to keep
your hand sewing supplies and notions together. Safely store
your favourite mug for travel. It's also the perfect hiding
place for precious toys and special treasures.

Finished Size
Approximately 6" (15 cm) high and 6
½" (16.5 cm) across the base.

Materials

✓ 13" (33cm) x width of fabric of plain fabric for the lining and bag side

✓ 7" (18cm) x width of fabric of floral fabric A for the bag base, side detail and casing

✓ 8" (20.5cm) x width of fabric of floral fabric B for the flower petals

✓ 40" (102cm) of pink ribbon ⅛" (3mm) wide

✓ 21" (53.5cm) of pink cotton lace trim ½" (12mm) wide

✓ 7" (18cm) x 27" (68.5cm) fusible fleece or wadding like Pellon Vilene

✓ 10" (25.5cm) x 3" (7.5cm) lightweight fusible interfacing

✓ 1 ½" (4cm) x 4" (10cm) pale blue wool felt for ribbon 'pulls'

✓ DMC floss in 3716 (very light dusty rose) and 519 (sky blue)

✓ Embroidery needle

✓ Bodkin or safety pin for threading ribbon through fabric casing

✓ Water erasable pen

✓ Leather 'handmade' label [2" (5cm) x ½" (12mm)] or other trim for decoration (optional)

✓ Iron and ironing board

✓ Rotary cutter, ruler and mat

✓ General sewing supplies

✓ Pretty Petal Dilly Bag template

TIP: Ensure fabrics are well pressed at each stage of the bag construction.

INSTRUCTIONS

1 Make the bag lining. Using the bag base template, cut one fabric circle from the lining fabric. Then cut one strip of fabric 7" (18cm) x 20 ⅝" (52.5cm). Place the short ends of the fabric strip together with right sides facing. Measure 1 ½" (3.5cm) from the top, and place a mark on the fabric edge using a water erasable marker. Repeat this process to draw a mark 1 ½" (3.5cm) from the bottom of the fabric also. (The space between these pen marks will remain unstitched so that it can be used as an opening to turn the bag right way out, when it's finished.) Using a ⅜" (1cm) seam allowance, sew a seam from the top of the fabric down to the 1 ½" (3.5cm) mark. Do the same from the bottom end of the fabric. Be sure to secure your stitching well with a few back stitches, as you start and finish each seam. You will now have a short tube with a 4" (10cm) opening in the centre.

2 Fold the tube flat so that the seam is on one side. Using the water erasable marker, place a mark at the opposite side to the seam, at the base of the fabric.

3 Fold this marked end toward the seam, and use this fold line to place two more marks on the base of either side of the fabric. The fabric tube will now be divided into four equal sections (or quarters).

4 Fold the circle base fabric in half and mark the edge of the circle on the fold lines. Fold the fabric again, to divide the circle into quarters. Mark the circle edge at the other two fold lines so that the whole circle is now marked into quarters.

5 Pin the fabric of one end of the tube to the fabric circle. Start by matching the quarter marks made on the fabric circle and tube and pin together. Continue to add many pins to help manoeuvre the tube around the circle. Sew the circle to the tube, using a ⅜" (1 cm) seam allowance (being sure to remove the pins as you go).

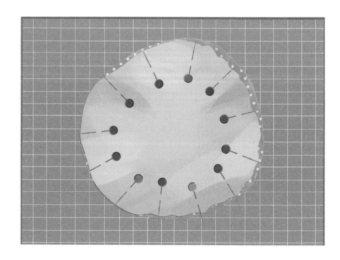

6 Clip the seam allowance up to the stitch line (being careful not to accidentally nick the seam). Set the lining aside for now.

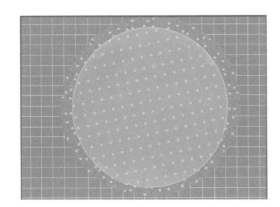

7 Make the bag base. Cut a circle of floral fabric A, using the circle template. Cut a circle of fusible fleece using the inner circle template. Follow the manufacturer's instructions to iron the fleece to the centre of the wrong side of the fabric circle. (To reduce bulk in the seam allowance, there is no fleece along the outer edge of the circle). Use the water erasable pen to mark the fabric base with cross hatched lines measuring 1" (2.5cm) apart. Using a thread colour to match the outer bag fabric, sew over these lines to quilt the bag base. Use a damp cloth to remove the pen marks, before pressing the base.

8 Cut a strip of plain fabric measuring 5" (12.5 cm) x 20 ⅝" (52.5 cm) for the bag side. Cut another strip of floral fabric A for the contrasting detail measuring 2 ¾" (7cm) x 20 ⅝" (52.5cm). With right sides facing, sew the two strips of fabric together along the long edge (using a ⅜" (1cm) seam allowance). Press the seam allowance towards the floral fabric.

9 Centre a 6 ¼" (16 cm) x 19 ⅞" (50.5 cm) piece of fusible fleece to the wrong side of the fabric strip and iron in place (following the manufacturer's instructions).

10 On the right side of the fabric strip, pin the length of lace over the seam, and stitch in place.

11 Measure ¼" (6mm) up from the lace, and rule a line with the water erasable marker. Using 6 strands of the dusty rose DMC floss, hand sew a running stitch along the line. Erase the marker line with a damp cloth once complete.

12 Sew a decorative leather label to the front of the fabric on the right hand side, using the same dusty rose DMC floss. Ensure the label is placed about 1 ½" (3.5 cm) from the right hand edge of the fabric and about ½" (12 mm) down from the top of the lace (depending on the label size).

13 Sew the petals for the bag. Using the petal template cut out six pairs of petal pieces - 12 pieces in total. Pin each pair together (with right sides facing) and trace the stitching line from the template on one side of each pair. Sew each pair together, following the stitching line, and leaving the straight side open at the top.

TIP: The stitching line helps ensure that all the petals are shaped identically.

14 Cut notches around the curved edge of the seam allowance, being careful not to clip the stitch line. Trim the seam allowance to ¼" (6mm).

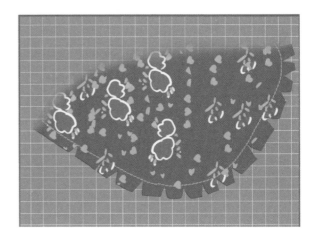

15 Turn the petals right way out, through the open end, and press.

16 Attach the petals to the fabric strip for the outer bag. Fold the bag fabric in half and use the water erasable pen to mark the half way point on the top of the fabric. Position the petals along the top of the fabric, starting at the centre mark. Pin in place leaving a very small gap between each petal. Ensure that the petals are not pinned over the 3/8" (1cm) seam allowance at each end of the fabric.

17 Baste stitch the petals in place with a straight stitch and a scant seam allowance of 1/8" (3 mm). Remove the pins as you sew.

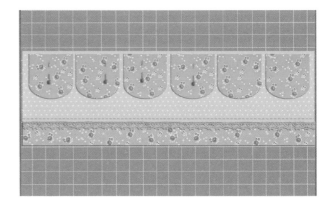

18 Sew the ribbon casing strips. Cut two strips of fabric A 10" (25.5 cm) long and 1 ½" (4 cm) wide. Cut two strips of fusible interfacing the same size. Attach the interfacing to the wrong side of the fabric (using the manufacturer's instructions). Fold the short ends of each fabric strip over by ¼" (6mm) to the wrong side and stitch a hem ⅛" (3mm) from the edge. Fold the strips in half lengthways (with right sides facing out) and press.

19 Place the open end of the casings along the top of the bag (over the petals) and pin in place. Ensure that the strips cover three petals and are separated in the centre of the bag with a small gap. Stitch in place with a scant ⅛" (3mm) seam allowance.

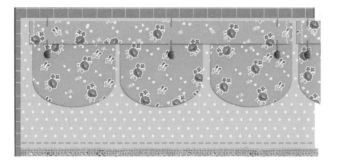

20 Fold the bag fabric in half (widthways) with right sides together and pin. Sew from the top to the bottom of the side with a ⅜" (1cm) seam allowance. The fusible fleece should end at the seam line. Be sure that the ribbon casings and petals aren't accidentally caught in the seam.

21 Follow the method used to sew the lining together, to stitch the outer bag tube to the quilted bag base. After marking the quarter points on the outer bag tube and the base, pin everything together with right sides facing.

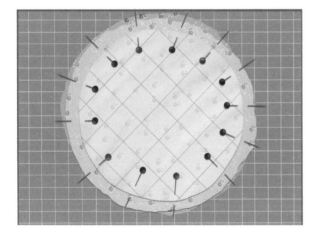

22 Sew the outer bag to the base using ⅜" (1cm) seam allowance. Then remove the sewing pins.

23 Cut notches into the seam allowance at close intervals to help the bag outer sit nicely when turned right way out. You may also wish to trim away some of the excess seam allowance.

24 Turn the bag right way out. Place the outer bag inside the lining so that right sides are facing. (The lining should still be facing the wrong way out.) Line up the two side seams then pin around the top of the bag, through the lining and bag outer (including the petals and bag casing which should still be facing down). If the tops of the bags don't quite match in circumference, now is the time to adjust the lining side seam (so that both the lining and bag are the same size and fit together nicely).

25 Using a small seam allowance, sew around the top edge of the bag (through the lining, casing, petals and bag fabric). Start at the side seam and be sure to stitch below the basting stitches sewn at ⅛" (3mm). Secure your stitching well with a short section of backstitching when you reach the place where you started sewing.

26 Pull the right side of the bag out through the gap in the side seam of the bag lining. Push the lining into the bag to ensure everything fits together neatly. When you're happy with the fit, gently pull the lining back out. Using a needle and thread, neatly blind stitch the opening in the lining closed. The Stitch Library has more details on blind stitch.

27 Cut the 40" (102cm) length of narrow ribbon in half and heat seal each end. Using a bodkin or safety pin, and starting at the side seam of the bag, thread the ribbon through one casing, and then the next casing, back to the starting point. Tie the ribbon ends together in a loose knot.

28 Now starting at the opposite side of the bag, repeat this process, so that you have a tied ribbon end at each side of the casings.

29 Decorate the knotted end of both ribbons with a felt leaf pull. Cut two pairs of felt leaf shapes from pale blue felt. Pin one pair of felt leaves over the knotted end of one of the ribbons. Blanket stitch the leaves together using two strands of sky blue DMC floss. See the Stitch Library for more on blanket stitch. Be sure to stitch through the ribbon to help hold it in place. Repeat this process for the other ribbon.

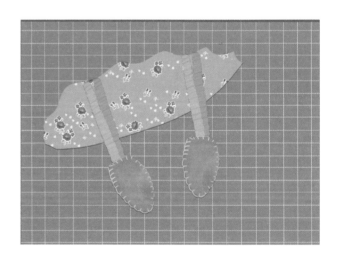

30 Pull the ribbon to draw the bag closed.

Quilted Carry All

The Quilted Carry All is just the right size for storing your sewing when you travel, for transporting your books to the library or for carrying those extra essentials that just won't fit in your purse. Made with an English paper pieced base and hand quilted hexagons, the extra special details make this simple design a stand out!

Finished Size
16" (40.5 cm) wide and 13" (33 cm) tall (not including the handles)

Materials

✔ *Twenty-five 4" (10cm) squares of different floral fabrics to make 25 hexagons (this project used five different prints)*

✔ *Two 17" (43cm) x 10" (25.5cm) pieces of natural coloured linen for the outer bag*

✔ *17" (43cm) x 29" (73.5cm) of floral fabric for the bag lining*

✔ *17" (43cm) x 30" (76cm) of light weight fusible fleece for the outer bag*

✔ *14" (35.5cm) x 12" (30.5cm) of natural coloured linen for the bag handles*

✔ *14" (35.5cm) x 3" (7.5cm) of light weight fusible fleece for the bag handles*

✔ *4" (10cm) square of light weight fusible fleece for the bag charm*

✔ *4" (10cm) square of light weight fusible interfacing for the bag charm*

✔ *4" (10cm) square of appliqué fusible bonding web for the feature hexagon*

✔ *9" (23cm) of ⅜" (1cm) wide cream grosgrain ribbon for the bag charm*

✔ *3 ½" (9cm) square of red wool felt for the bag charm*

✔ *3 ½" (9cm) square of pink wool felt for the bag charm*

✔ *8" (20.5cm) x 2" (5cm) piece of cream wool felt for the bag charm*

✔ *DMC floss in Ecru*

✔ *Water erasable pen*

✔ *Quilted Carry All template*

✔ *Blossom Scissor Charm template (for the bag charm)*

✔ *Thick paper to create twenty-six 2" hexagon paper shapes*

✔ *Glue basting pen*

✔ *60 weight polyester bobbin thread in white, grey or beige*

✔ *Milliner's needle in size 9*

✔ *Leather label or other trim for decoration (optional)*

✔ *Rotary cutter, acrylic patchwork ruler and self healing mat*

✔ *General sewing supplies*

TIP: When machine sewing, this project is best stitched using a walking foot.

INSTRUCTIONS

1 Use the template provided to trace and cut 26 identical 2" hexagon paper shapes. Put one paper aside to use as a tracing template later.

2 Glue-baste two hexagons in the same floral fabric for the bag charm. Set aside.

3 Glue-baste one hexagon to be used as a feature on the linen panel on one side of the bag. Ensure the top of the hexagon is a point. Set aside.

SEW THE OUTER BAG

4 Glue-baste 22 hexagons, using a range of the five different floral fabrics. For more detailed instructions on making and sewing hexagons, see English Paper Piecing Techniques at the beginning of the book.

5 Create a hexagon panel that will form the base of the outer bag. Arrange the 22 hexagons so that the sides are flat and the points are facing the top and bottom. The rows will contain the following number of hexagons from top to bottom;

First row: 6, Second row: 5, Third row: 6, Bottom Row: 5

If you have prints that are directional, ensure the hexagons in the first and second rows are right way up, and the hexagons in the third and fourth rows are upside down.

6 When you are happy with the layout, photograph your panel so that you can refer to the image as you stitch.

7 Whip stitch the hexagon panel together using a single strand of fine bobbin thread and a fine milliner's needle. You'll find more details about whip stitch in the Stitch Library.

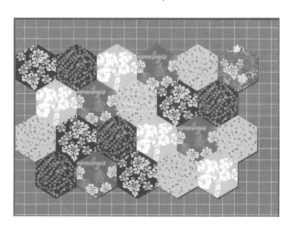

8 Remove the hexagon papers from the back of the panel, starting with those in the centre. Press the panel as you go, to help keep the hexagons in shape.

9 Trim the panel using a rotary cutter, acrylic patchwork ruler and self healing mat, so that it measures 17" wide and 11" high. Ensure that it is centred and that your hexagon seams are straight or square.

10 Using a ¼" (6mm) seam allowance, join each of the linen panels to the top and bottom of the trimmed hexagon panel (along the 17" sides). Press the seams open. This will form the Outer Bag panel.

11 Following the manufacturer's instructions, secure the 17" (43cm) x 30" (76cm) piece of light weight fusible fleece to the wrong side of the bag panel. You may also wish to sew a baste stitch along the raw edges of the hexagon panel, about 1/8" (3mm) from the fabric edge. This will help keep the hexagon stitching intact.

12 Use a 2" hexagon paper (the one put aside earlier) and a water erasable pen to trace the outline of the hexagon shapes onto both linen panels on either side of the hexagon panel. Follow the lines of the hand stitched hexagons to determine the placement of the hexagon template.

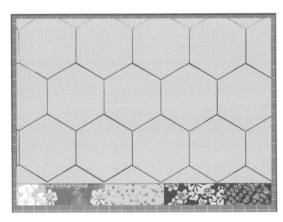

13 Remove the backing paper from the single hexagon made as a feature for the linen panel. Press the hexagon.

14 Use the paper hexagon template to trace the hexagon shape onto the paper side of the square of fusible bonding web. Cut out the shape so that it is slightly smaller than the hexagon template.

15 Place the fusible webbing hexagon onto the wrong side of the fabric 'feature' hexagon so that the paper side is facing out. Secure with a warm iron, and then peel off the backing paper.

16 Position the hexagon over one of the traced hexagon shapes in the middle row on the right hand side of one of the linen panels. Secure in place with a warm iron. Be careful not to iron the erasable marker lines though, as the heat will set the lines in place.

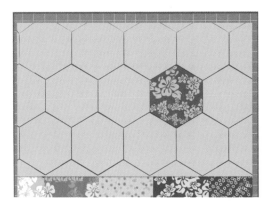

17 Using a single strand of bobbin thread, sew the hexagon in place using small, fine blind stitches. See the Stitch Library for more details on all the different stitch types.

18 Thread a needle with three strands of Ecru DMC floss. Hand quilt over the traced hexagon lines on the linen, using a small fine running stitch. When all lines are quilted, remove the erasable pen lines with a damp cloth.

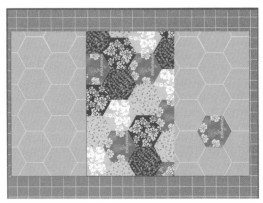

19 Add a leather label to the right hand side of the hexagon panel (on the opposite side of the panel with the feature hexagon). Stitch it in place with six strands of Ecru DMC floss. Position it just below the seam line and ensure it's centred inside a hexagon shape.

20 Press the Outer Bag panel. Fold in half with right sides facing and pin along the sides. Ensure the side seams between the hexagon panel and the linen are aligned on either side.

21 Stitch down each side using a ⅜" (1cm) seam allowance.

22 Box the corners on the base of the Outer Bag. Measure and mark a 1 inch square on both the bottom corners. Measure 1" in from the seam line, and 1" from the base (on the fold). Cut away the square of fabric on both corners.

23 Pinch the corners so that the seam line is centred and the raw edges line up.

24 Stitch across both corner seams using a ¼" (6mm) seam allowance. Turn the Outer Bag right way out. Set aside.

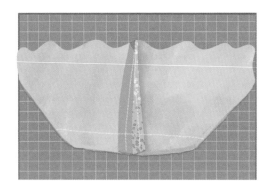

SEW THE BAG LINING

TIP: The Bag Lining fabric is cut slightly shorter than the Outer Bag fabric to reduce puckering inside the bag.

25 Fold the 17" (43cm) x 29" (73.5cm) bag lining fabric in half with right sides facing. Pin along the short sides.

26 Stitch down one side using a ⅜" (1cm) seam allowance.

27 On the other side, measure 4" (10cm) down from the raw edges on the top of the lining and mark a line on the fabric edge. Measure down another 5" (12.5cm) and make another mark. Using a ⅜" (1cm) seam allowance, sew the side seam of the lining from the top of the lining to the 4" (10cm) mark. Secure the seam with a short row of back stitch. Then sew the second part of the seam from the next mark (at 9" (23cm) from the top of the lining) to the base of the lining (on the fold). Again, back stitch the beginning and end of the seam. This will leave you with a 5" (12.5cm) opening in the seam (which will be used for turning the bag right way out when complete).

28 Box both the corners of the bag lining using the steps outlined in steps 22 – 24. Do not turn the lining right way out. Set aside.

SEW THE BAG HANDLES

29 Cut four strips of linen measuring 14" (35.5cm) x 3" (7.5cm). Cut two strips of fusible fleece measuring 14" (35.5cm) x 1½" (3.8cm).

30 Follow the manufacturer's instructions to secure the two strips of fusible fleece onto the centre of the wrong side of two of the linen strips.

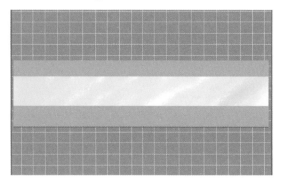

31 Fold the edges of both fabric strips over the interfacing and towards the centre of the fabric, and press.

32 Fold the two remaining linen strips in half lengthways and press. Open the strips out, then fold the right sides of the fabric strips over to meet this pressed centre line.

33 Pair each interfaced fabric strip with a folded fabric strip. This will form your two bag handles. Place both strips of fabric with their folded sides together and pin.

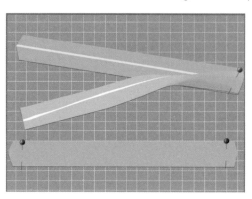

34 Using a thread colour to match your linen, sew down each long side of the handles to join the two strips of fabric together. Use a ¼" (6mm) seam allowance. Sew three more evenly spaced seams between the two outside seam lines approximately ¼" (6mm) apart.

TIP: For super straight and evenly spaced stitches, use a ruler and water erasable pen to mark the seam lines before you sew.

35 Pin the handles to the Outer Bag. Lay the Outer Bag down flat. Use a clear acrylic patchwork ruler and a water erasable pen to mark the centre of the bag along the top raw edge. Measure and mark 2½" (5cm) on either side from this centre mark. Turn the bag over and repeat on the other side. Ensure the marks are positioned in the same place on both sides of the bag.

36 Pin both the handles to the bag by aligning the raw edges on the end of the handles with the raw edge on the top of the bag. Place each handle on the outside of the marked lines. Pin in place with at least two pins to help keep the handles straight when sewing the bag together.

TIP: You may also wish to baste stitch the handles in place using a scant ⅛" (3mm) seam allowance.

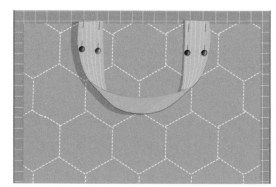

37 Place the Outer Bag inside the Bag Lining so that their right sides are facing. Ensure the handles facing down between the Outer Bag and the Lining too. Align the side seams and pin right around the top of the bag (pinning the side seams open). If the Outer Bag and Lining do not match up perfectly, make adjustments now to ensure they are both exactly the same size and that they pin together neatly without any puckering.

38 Stitch around the top of the bag using a ⅜" (1cm) seam allowance. Remove the sewing pins as you go. Reverse stitch over the handles to reinforce them.

39 Turn the bag the right way out by pulling the Outer Bag through the turning gap in the lining.

40 Push the lining into the Outer Bag. You may also wish to press it in place.

41 Top stitch around the top of bag, using a ¼" (6mm) seam allowance. Start at one side seam and sew around the entire top of the bag, back stitching when you reach the starting point.

42 Blind stitch the turning hole in the bag lining closed. Use a doubled strand of coordinating thread for extra strength. Push the lining back down into the bag.

MAKE THE BAG CHARM

43 The felt flower for the bag charm is made using the same template as the Blossom Scissor Charm. Refer to those instructions for more detail on the following steps. Use the flower template to cut a pink felt flower and a red felt flower shape. Place both shapes together with the pink flower shape on top. Use the rolled centre template to cut the cream felt. Follow the instructions to stitch the rolled centre felt together with cream thread. Place the base of the rolled centre into the centre hole in the top of the felt flowers and whip stitch them together from the back.

44 Using the paper hexagon template, trace the hexagon shape onto the 4" squares of fusible fleece and fusible interfacing. Cut out both shapes slightly smaller than the traced lines.

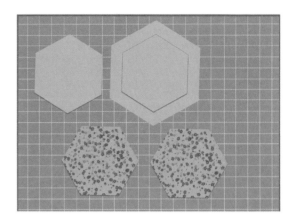

45 Remove the backing papers from the two hexagons you made earlier for the bag charm and press them both.

46 Press the fusible fleece to the wrong side of one hexagon and the fusible interfacing to the wrong side of the other hexagon.

47 Sew the felt flower to the centre right side of the hexagon backed with fusible fleece. Use small, fine stitches that cannot be seen from the front of the flower. Choose sewing thread colours that match your felt.

48 Place the two hexagons together with wrong sides facing. Use the milliner's needle and a single strand of bobbin thread to whip stitch four sides of the hexagons together. Keep the thread intact for the next step.

49 Loop the ribbon around the left hand side of the bag handle (on the side of the bag without the feature hexagon). Place both ribbon ends into the opening of the hexagon so that each piece of ribbon sits at either side of the hexagon point. Pin the ribbons in place. Continue to whip stitch the remaining two sides of the hexagons together (sewing through the ribbon as you go).

50 Use three strands of Ecru DMC floss to quilt around the outside edge of the hexagons with a fine running stitch.

Sweet Treat Wall Banner

Picture
this dainty wall banner
brightening up a pastel baby nursery
or adding a delicious accent in the kitchen.
This is the ideal beginner's project, introducing you to
a range of techniques including appliqué, hand stitching
and embroidery, making fabric yoyo's, working with felt and
machine sewing too. It uses a mix of materials and is also
really versatile. The cupcake looks delicious, but perhaps
you'd like to try something different.
Change the appliqué or the embellishments!

Finished Size
The completed fabric banner
will measure approximately 11 ½"
(29cm) long and 8 ¼" (21cm) wide

Materials

✓ 9" (23cm) x 19" (48.5cm) white fabric like duck cloth, linen or quilter's cotton

✓ 9" (23cm) x 6" (15cm) floral fabric like Liberty

✓ 3" (8cm) square of fabric like Liberty for the yoyo

✓ Paper backed fusible appliqué web like Vliesofix

✓ 4" (10cm) x 2½" (6.5cm) almond felt

✓ 5½" (14cm) x 4" (10cm) white felt

✓ 4½" (11.5cm) x 3" (7.5cm) pale pink felt

✓ 21" (53.5cm) pink crochet lace trim - ⅜" (1cm) wide

✓ Small decorative button

✓ 20" (51cm) of ⅛" (3mm) wide grosgrain ribbon

✓ DMC floss – 210 (MD lavender), 3864 (LT mocha beige), B5200 (snow white), Ecru (ecru), 3713 (V LT salmon), 603 (cranberry), 800 (pale delft blue),

✓ Embroidery needle

✓ 10" (25.5cm) of ⅜" (10mm) diameter timber dowel rod

✓ Water erasable pen

✓ Ballpoint pen

✓ Patchwork ruler

✓ Pinking shears (zig zag scissors) - optional

✓ Sweet treat cupcake template and tracing paper

✓ General sewing supplies

INSTRUCTIONS

NOTE: *The seam allowance for this project is ⅜" (1cm) unless stated otherwise.*

1 Trace the banner template onto paper. Pin the template over the floral fabric so that the point is at the bottom. Trace and cut out the fabric shape on the line. Remove the template.

2 Pin the floral fabric from step 1 over one end of the white fabric so that the point lines up with the fabric base. Trace the diagonal lines onto the white fabric using a water erasable marker. Cut the fabric on the line to make a point.

3 Lay the two pieces of fabric with right sides together along the short straight edge (opposite the points). Pin in place and then stitch this straight edge.

4 Press the seam allowance down towards the floral fabric. Fold the fabric in half (with wrong sides facing) so that the two points meet up. Press the fabric to create a fold line across the top. Set aside for now.

5 Appliqué the felt cupcake. For help with Appliqué, see the Appliqué Techniques at the front of the book. Trace the three cupcake shapes onto the paper side of the fusible webbing and roughly cut around the outside of each shape.

6 Iron the fusible webbing to one side of the felt; almond for the base, white for the top and pink for the icing.

TIP: For all felt work, use a press cloth to protect the felt from the heat of the iron.

7 Cut out the templates on the line. Peel off the backing paper.

8 Position the cupcake on the banner fabric. Centre the cupcake base so that it is overlapping the floral fabric by about 3/8" (1cm). Press in place. Place the white top over the base so that the scallops just overlap it. Press in place. Position the pink icing over the top of the white top and press to secure.

9 Hand appliqué the cupcake and embroider the details. For more details on specific stitch types, please see the Stitch Library. First use a ruler and water erasable marker to rule vertical lines on the cupcake base. Use the photograph as a guide.

10 Using two strands of light mocha beige DMC floss and an embroidery needle, sew a fine running stitch around the outside edge of the cupcake base. Then sew a running stitch along every second line marked on the cupcake base. Change to two strands of Ecru DMC floss and continue to running stitch the remaining lines.

11 Blanket stitch around the outside edge of the white felt using two strands of snow white DMC floss.

12 Sew a fine running stitch around the entire icing shape, using two strands of very light salmon DMC floss.

13 Use the water erasable marker to randomly draw short lines (⅛" or 3mm long) on the top of the icing to represent sprinkles (decorative sweets).

14 Embroider these lines using three strands of DMC floss in randomly placed colours (from the materials list).

15 Use the water erasable marker and a ruler to draw a line on the floral fabric (on either side of the cupcake base) that is around ¼" or 6mm below the seam line. Sew a running stitch along this line using three strands of lavender DMC floss.

16 Use a ruler to measure ¾" or 2cm from the top fold line. Mark this line with the water erasable marker. Unfold the banner fabric and open it out flat with the right side facing you. Cut a 9" (23cm) length of lace. Position it on the fabric so that the top of the lace sits on the marked line. Pin in place before sewing a straight line across the top of the lace to secure.

17 Use a damp cloth or remove all water erasable lines on the front of the banner. Then press the banner fabric on the wrong side.

18 Make a fabric yoyo for the cupcake decoration. Trace the circle from the template onto paper and cut out. Pin the template to the 3" (8cm) square of fabric and trace the outline with a water erasable marker. Cut out.

19 Double thread an embroidery needle with sewing cotton and tie a knot in the end. Fold over a scant 1/8" (or 3mm) hem and sew a neat, even running stitch around the outside of the circle.

20 When you have completed 'hemming the circle', ensure that the last stitch exits on the right side of the fabric. Gently pull the thread to gather up the stitches into a little puff.

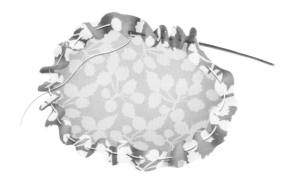

21 Flatten the puff and then shape the yoyo with your fingers, helping the 'pleats' to be evenly spaced. When you're happy with the shape, sew extra stitches to secure the yoyo. Sew down through the pleats and through to the wrong side of the yoyo, then back up through the centre. Ensure these stitches are small and hidden amongst the fabric pleats. Trim off the excess thread.

22 Position the yoyo on the top right of the cupcake at the top of the icing. Using two strands of the lavender DMC floss, sew the yoyo in place with a few stitches in the centre. Place a decorative button over the centre of the yoyo and stitch in place.

23 Fold the banner fabric in half with right sides facing. Using a water erasable marker and ruler, mark the seam line ⅜" (1cm) in from the fabric edge. This line will start at the lace seam line, go down the one side and around the base. On the opposite side, rule a line 2" (5cm) down from the lace seam line. Leave a 3 ½" (9cm) space, and then continue to rule the line. The space will be our turning gap.

TIP: Marking the seam lines directly onto the fabric helps ensure that you don't sew through the sections that need to remain unstitched, including the area above the lace seam line!

24 Pin the banner fabric together ready for sewing. Sew the seam lines marked (being careful to leave open both the space above the lace seam and the turning gap). Remove pins.

25 Trim the seam allowance with pinking shears or scissors to ¼" (6mm).

26 Use the turning gap to carefully turn the banner right way out ensuring all the corners are neat. Press the seams flat (including the turning gap opening and the open seams above the lace trim).

27 Top stitch around the sides and top of the banner about 1/8" or 3mm from the fabric edge. Start at the base of one side, stitch up to the top of the lace (not to the top of the banner). Sew along the top of the lace and then back down the other side. This top stitching will sew the turning gap closed, but will leave an opening at the top of the banner to insert a dowel rod.

28 Pin the remaining lace to the base of the point (being careful to fold the raw edges under at each end). Top stitch the lace in place. Start sewing from the point in the centre and stitch out to one side. Repeat for the other side.

29 Thread the dowel rod through the top of the banner.

30 Make a hanging loop by tying the length of ribbon to either end of the dowel rod. Now your pretty banner is all ready for hanging!

Posie Patchwork Pouch

The Posie Patchwork Pouch features a pretty lace zipper, crochet lace trims, hand quilted details, simple patchwork and a clever boxed design. You can also add the most adorable little felt flower zipper pull. It's perfectly sized for use as a make up pouch, or to store your pencils and art supplies.

Finished Size
9" (23cm) long x 4 ½" (11.5cm)
wide x 3 ½" (9 cm) high

Materials

✓ Six 12" (30.5cm) x 2 ½" (6cm) rectangles of different fabrics (I used six shades of Liberty lawn in Betsy)

✓ Two 12 ½" (32cm) x 2 ½" (6cm) rectangles of blue linen

✓ 6" (15cm) x 2" (5cm) of fabric for the tab

✓ 16" (41cm) x 12 ½" (32cm) of fusible fleece or wadding like Pellon Vilene

✓ 16" (41cm) x 12 ½" (32cm) of natural coloured linen for the lining

✓ Two 12.5" (32cm) lengths of ⅜" (1cm) wide natural coloured, cotton crochet lace trim

✓ 6" (15cm) of 1 ⅜" (3.5cm) wide natural coloured, cotton crochet lace trim

✓ 12" (30cm) lace zip in natural

✓ Felt scraps in pale blue, pale pink and pale green

✓ Freezer paper scraps

✓ DMC floss in Ecru, 3713 (very light salmon), 800 (pale delft blue)

✓ Embroidery needle

✓ Water erasable marker

✓ Flower Zipper Pull template

✓ General sewing supplies

NOTE: All seam allowances for this project are ¼" (6mm) unless stated otherwise.

TIP: This project is best stitched with a walking foot on your sewing machine. Change to a zipper foot to attach the lace zip.

INSTRUCTIONS

1 Use a rotary cutter, ruler and mat to accurately cut all fabric strips and pieces as outlined in the materials list.

2 Make the side tabs for the pouch. Cut the 6" (15 cm) of crochet lace trim in half widthways, to make two 3" (7.5 cm) long strips.

3 Fold the 6" (15 cm) x 2" (5 cm) strip of fabric in half lengthways and press. Fold both the outside raw edges into the centre (with the right side of the fabric facing out) and press. Cut the strip of folded fabric into two 3" (7.5 cm) long strips.

4 Cut the 1 ⅜" (3.5cm) wide piece of lace in half to create two 3" (7.5cm) pieces. Centre the fabric strips over the lace (with right side facing out) and pin in place. Top stitch down both sides of each piece.

5 Fold each strip in half and sew along the raw edges of the width (using a scant ⅛" (3 mm) seam allowance, to create two tabs for the pouch. Set aside.

6 Join the six fabric strips together (along the length) using a ¼" (6 mm) seam allowance. Press the fabric panel seams open.

7 Sew the two linen strips to each end of the fabric panel.

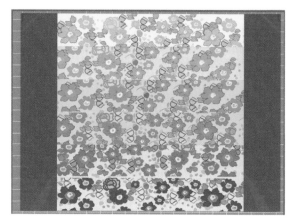

8 Iron the fusible fleece to the wrong side of the panel (following the manufacturer's instructions).

9 With the water erasable marker, rule a line along both the linen fabric strips ⅜" (1 cm) in from the seam. Pin the two 12.5" (32 cm) lengths of cotton crochet lace onto the linen (at each end of the panel) so that the base of the lace rests on the marked line and the top of the lace faces the raw fabric edge. Sew in place.

10 Using three strands of Ecru DMC floss, hand sew a running stitch between the base of the lace trim and the seam line.

11 With a clear patchwork ruler and water erasable pen, mark a diagonal line from the top left corner of the

floral centre panel to the bottom right corner. Then mark lines on either side of this central line at 1 ½" (3.5 cm) intervals. Mark a diagonal line across the opposite corners. And again mark diagonal lines at 1 ½" (3.5 cm) intervals. This cross-hatched quilting design is all ready for stitching.

12 Using two strands of Ecru DMC floss, hand quilt the panel with running stitch. Remove the marker pen lines with a damp cloth once all the stitching is complete.

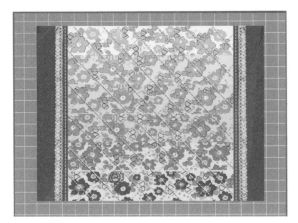

13 Place the quilted panel and the linen lining fabric together with right sides facing. Sew the lining to the panel straight along the linen ends using a ¼" (6 mm) seam allowance. Leave the top and bottom open.

14 Turn the panel right way out. Press, then baste stitch the panel and lining together along the top and bottom of the panel, using a scant ⅛" (3 mm) seam allowance.

15 Place the panel right side up on a flat surface. Pin one side of the lace zipper in place along the top edge of one side of the linen (covering the linen and lining seam). Ensure that the zip is closed, centred and that the metal zipper ends are equally spaced from the fabric ends. Test the zipper before you sew it in place, to ensure it opens easily without catching on the fabric.

16 Sew the zipper in place along the pinned side about ⅛" (3 mm) from the centre of the zip. It's easier to start at the zipper base. Check as you sew to be sure you catch the fabric in the seam underneath. Use a zipper foot, as it will help you navigate around the zipper pull and help you to sew close to the zipper edge. You may need to alter the needle position to sew close to the zip though. Alternatively, use a walking foot to start stitching the zip down. When you reach the zipper pull, ensure the needle is positioned in the fabric. Lift the presser foot lever and slide the zipper pull (to open the zip) past the sewing machine foot. Lower the lever to continue sewing the zipper in place.

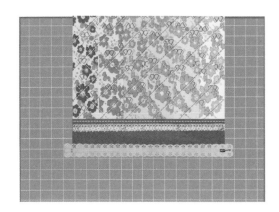

17 When you have sewn one side in place, close the zipper, and pin the other side of the pouch in place. Ensure that the fabric ends line up evenly. Sew the seam following the instructions in the previous step. Do a final test to check that the zipper is operational. You now have a tube with the zipper attached.

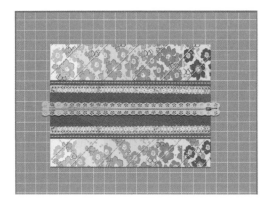

18 With the zip open (and a couple of inches from the end), turn the tube so that the lining is facing out. Press the tube flat so that the lace zip is positioned across the centre. Position the two folded tabs (made at the beginning) so that they are facing in and are centred under the zipper on each side of tube. The raw edges of the tabs will line up with the raw edges of the tube. Pin the tabs in place and pin the sides together. Sew each side seam of the tube with a ⅜" (1 cm) seam allowance, being careful to sew on the inside edge of the metal ends of the zip. Back stitch over the tab and zip seams to reinforce this area.

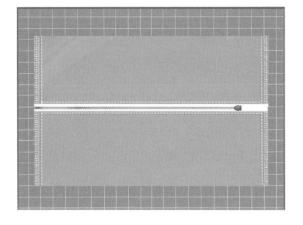

19 Turn the pouch right way out just to ensure the seams and tabs are all correct before finishing the seams. Turn the pouch inside out again, then overlock, serge or zig zag stitch the raw edges. (If you're an experienced sewist, your finish for the interior may include binding these interior seams for a neater finish.)

20 To box the pouch corners, pinch the corner so that the side seam is centred and the corner forms a triangle. Measure down 1 ½" (4 cm) from the corner point and pin. Check the inside of pouch to ensure that the pin is positioned just beside the seam of the blue linen trim. It's important to make sure the seam will be straight and square with the seams on the outside of the pouch. Once you are happy with the pin position use a ruler and water erasable marker to rule a line straight across the pin mark. Do this for all four corners ensuring that the ruled lines are the same length for all (and the boxed seams will look the same for all when the pouch is turned right way out).

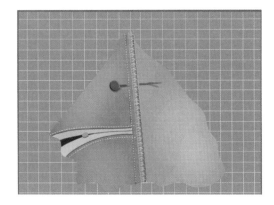

21 Sew along the lines for each corner.

22 Turn the pouch right way out to make sure the seams are straight and the pouch is neatly boxed. Then turn inside out again to trim and then overlock, serge or zig zag these corner seams.

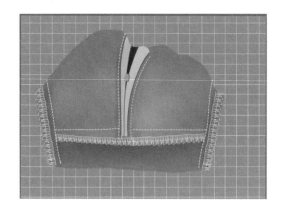

23 Turn the pouch right way out.

24 To make the felt flower zipper pull, trace the flower, flower centre and leaf shape onto freezer paper. Iron the freezer paper onto felt scraps to create two pink flower shapes, two pale blue flower centres and two green leaves. See the section about Working With Felt for more details.

25 Using two strands of blue DMC floss, sew the flower centres to the middle of the flower shapes with a fine running stitch.

26 Pin the flowers together with wrong sides facing, and the petals aligned. Overlap the two leaf shapes and place the ends between the two flower shapes. Blanket stitch around the outside of the two flowers using two strands of very light salmon DMC floss. The Stitch Library has more details on blanket stitch. Sew through the two leaves as you go. Sew four petals together first. Insert the round end of the lace zipper into the space where the 5th petals are. Then continue to blanket stitch around these petals, catching the metal zipper pull as you sew.

TIP: Add other finishing touches to make the Posie Patchwork Pouch your own. Sew decorative buttons to the tabs, a leather tag to the side, or add a pretty charm to the zipper pull.

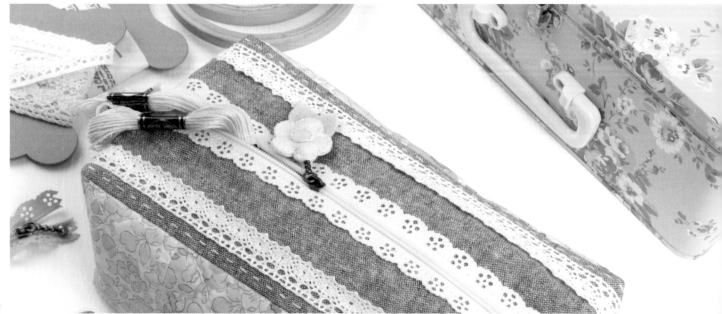

Hoppy Squares Table Tidy

It's a happy, hoppy bunny that adorns the front
of this generously sized placemat. Tiny florals and
pretty pastels work wonderfully with this design. But
bold, bright colours would be a striking look too. Combining
appliqué, hand quilting, embroidery and patchwork, this
pattern includes a couple of clever time saving tricks. So it's
a wonderful introduction
to all of these techniques.

Finished Size
The finished table tidy is
approximately 20 ½" (52cm)
across and 12 ½" (31.8cm) high.

Materials

✓ Cream wool felt for the bunny appliqué

✓ Wool felt scraps in pale pink, pale peach and pale blue for the bunny appliqué

✓ 3 ½" (9cm) x 1 ¼" (3cm) fine floral for the bunny collar appliqué

✓ 10" (25.4cm) square of floral fabric for the scalloped border

✓ 14" (35.5cm) square of fine pin dot fabric for the appliqué background

✓ Twelve 5" (12.7cm) x 2 ½" (6.4cm) rectangles of coordinating floral fabric for the patchwork panels (cut two each from six prints)

✓ 20 ½" (52cm) x 12 ½" (31.8cm) floral fabric for the placemat backing

✓ 22 ½" (57cm) x 14 ½" (37cm) polyester quilt wadding or fusible fleece

✓ Paper backed fusible appliqué bonding web like Vliesofix

✓ 67" (170cm) pale pink crochet lace trim (⅜" or 10mm wide)

✓ DMC floss - Ecru, 818 (baby pink), 3713 (very light salmon), 3790 (ultra dark beige grey)

✓ Embroidery needle

✓ Press cloth

✓ Fine tracing paper or tissue paper and pen

✓ Rotary cutter, acrylic patchwork ruler and self healing cutting mat

✓ Water or heat erasable marking pen

✓ Quilt basting spray

✓ Hoppy Squares Table Tidy templates

✓ General sewing supplies including sewing machine

NOTE: All seam allowances for this project are ¼" (6mm) unless stated otherwise.

INSTRUCTIONS

APPLIQUÉ THE BUNNY SQUARE

1 Trace the individual pattern pieces onto the paper side of the fusible webbing for appliqué and roughly cut around each piece. The template has already been reversed so it appears as a mirror image of the completed bunny.

To make the scalloped border, fold the fusible webbing in half and trace the template, matching the fold lines on the template against the folded edge of the webbing.

For more information on appliqué see the 'Appliqué Techniques' section at the front of the book.

2 Iron each piece of fusible webbing to the wrong side of your chosen felt or fabrics for each of the appliqué shapes. Use a press cloth to cover the wool felt to avoid any heat damage. Then cut out the designs on the line.

3 Peel the backing paper off the collar and position it over the bunny body shape. Use a warm iron to secure it in place.

4 Peel the backing paper off the inner ears and centre them over the bunny ear shapes and iron to secure (covering the felt with a press cloth).

5 Peel the backing paper off all remaining felt appliqué shapes.

Ensure the square polka dot panel is pressed. Using the template as a guide, arrange each of the felt appliqué pieces onto the centre of the panel. Remember that the ears will be a mirror image of the template.

Place the pieces in the following order;
•Place neck piece down first
•Overlap body with collar over the bottom of the neck piece
•Overlap face over the top of the neck piece
•Tuck bottom of ears under the top of the head
•Overlap folded ear over side of ear shape
•Position nose and cheeks

When you are happy with the layout, cover the felt with a press cloth and use a warm iron to secure the pieces in place.

6 Fold the scalloped fabric border in half to find the centre top and bottom and press gently with your fingers. Fold the bunny fabric in half to find the vertical centre line and gently finger press. Peel the backing paper off the scalloped border and centre it over the bunny, lining up the fold lines. The border will slightly overlap the bottom of the bunny body and the tops of the ears. Press.

7 Appliqué around the raw edges of the felt and fabric shapes using your preferred method. Use sewing thread to match your fabric and felt colours. I used a small blanket stitch to sew the white felt first; the sides of the neck, the ears, then the head. Next, stitch the body and collar.

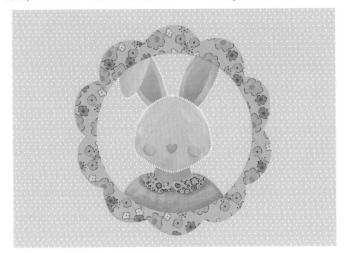

8 Appliqué the scalloped border.

TIP: Use a clear acrylic appliqué foot on the sewing machine to help you see your stitching.

9 Hand stitch some extra details on the bunny using two strands of DMC floss. Use pale pink floss to whip stitch the nose with small, fine stitches. Use the salmon floss to whip stitch around the peach cheeks and the inner ears. See the 'Stitch Library' for more tips on whip stitch.

10 Use a pen to trace the face details from the template onto a piece of tracing or tissue paper.

11 Cut around the face on the line (but leave the whiskers intact). Pin the template onto the bunny face being sure to line up the nose and cheeks.

12 Use two strands of pink floss to back stitch the mouth detail by sewing straight through the paper template and following the drawn lines. Then use two strands of beige grey to back stitch the whiskers and eyes.

13 When you've finished stitching, hold the stitches with one hand as you gently tear away the paper with the other. Tease any stray pieces of paper out from under the stitches with your needle (if necessary).

14 Press the finished bunny panel from the back. Then trim the panel down to a 12 ½" (31.8cm) square, being careful to centre the scalloped border design in the centre. Set aside.

SEW THE PATCHWORK SIDES

15 Arrange each of the twelve floral panels into two rows (with long sides together) and place one print in each row (and none of the same prints opposite each other). Photograph your fabric arrangement so you can refer to the image as you sew.

16 Sew the fabrics in each row together. Press seams open.

17 Use the same process to sew the second patchwork panel together. Each completed panel should be 12 ½" (31.8cm) long.

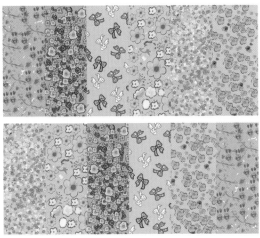

18 Carefully cut down the centre of each panel making four panels 2 ½" (6.4cm) wide.

19 Swap the panels so that you have two pairs with a panel from each. Sew each pair together (making sure to match up the seams of each of the squares). Press the seam open at the back.

20 Place the patchwork square panels on either sides of the bunny panel. Turn one panel upside down so that the squares appear in a different order to the opposite panel.

21 Sew each patchwork square panel to the side of the bunny panel by placing right sides together. Press the seam allowance towards the patchwork square panels then press the front of the panel (being sure to use a press cloth over the felt).

22 Use quilt basting spray to adhere the piece of polyester wadding to the wrong side of the panel. It will be larger than the panel to aid the quilting process. Alternatively use an iron to secure fusible fleece to the wrong side of the panel.

23 Use a ruler and a water or heat erasable marker to draw quilting lines onto the panel front. Draw a line ¼" (6mm) in from the side seam between the bunny and patchwork square panels on both sides. Draw diagonal lines to form cross hatches inside each of the patchwork squares. Note that there is a ¼" seam allowance still remaining around the outside edges of the mat. Don't include this border when positioning your quilting lines.

24 Carefully draw a free hand curved line ¼" (6mm) from the scalloped border edge.

25 Hand quilt all lines using three strands of Ecru floss and a fine, neat running stitch. Remove the lines after quilting. Press the panel.

26 Use a rotary cutter, mat and ruler to trim down the panel to remove the excess wadding / fusible fleece. It will measure 20 ½" (52cm) across and 12 ½" (31.8 cm) high.

27 Pin the lace right side down on the right side of the panel. Start at one corner and leave a small overhang. Continue around the panel, guiding the lace around each corner. There will be a small overhang at the end as well.

28 Using a scant ⅛" (3 mm) seam allowance, sew the lace to the panel. Start ⅛" (3 mm) in from the first corner. Be careful not the catch the extra pleat of lace in each corner. Stop ⅛" (3mm) in from the last corner. Remove the sewing pins.

29 Pin back the two lengths of lace at the corner join so that the folds overlap slightly.

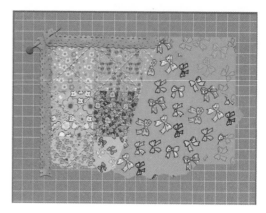

30 Pin the backing piece of floral fabric to the top of the panel so that right sides are facing. Both pieces of fabric should be exactly the same size.

31 Sew the panels together using a ¼" (6mm) seam allowance. Leave an 8" (20cm) opening at one of the patchwork ends to use as a turning gap. Backstitch at the start and finish of your stitching on either side of the turning gap. Be careful not to catch the pleat of lace (from each corner) in the seam. Remove the pins.

32 Trim each of the corners close to the seam line to remove extra bulk. Turn the fabric right way out. Use a chopstick, knitting needle or similar tool to help push out the corners.

33 Press the back of the table tidy, being careful to turn under the seam allowance at the turning gap.

34 Use a single strand of coordinating sewing thread to blind stitch the opening closed. Use the Stitch Library for more information on blind stitching.

35 Give the table tidy a final press and she's all ready to pretty up your dining space.

103

DIFFICULTY LEVEL
CONFIDENT BEGINNER

Bloom Cushion Cover

This English paper pieced cushion cover is the
perfect piece to brighten up a guest room or alfresco
setting. The flower shaped design showcases the delicate
hand embroidery in the centre. This 'scrap busting' project
is perfect for using up those beautiful treasured prints you
may have saved in your fabric stash. With no zips and an
envelope opening on the back, this project is
easier than it looks!

Finished Size
Approximately 15"
(38cm) x 15" (38cm)

Materials

- ✓ 15" (38cm) square of pale cotton fabric for cushion front

- ✓ 15" (38cm) square of fusible fleece or wadding like Pellon Vilene

- ✓ 15" (38cm) square of pale quilter's cotton backing fabric for the cushion front

- ✓ Two 15" (38cm) x 11" (28cm) pieces of quilter's cotton fabric for the envelope cushion back

- ✓ 6" (15cm) square of pale quilter's cotton fabric for the central embroidered hexagon

- ✓ 4" (10cm) timber embroidery hoop

- ✓ 4" x WOF (width of fabric) for binding fabric

- ✓ 13" (33cm) square of paper backed fusible appliqué webbing

- ✓ Fabric 1 quilter's cotton scraps for six 2" equilateral triangles

- ✓ Fabric 2 quilter's cotton scraps for twelve 1" jewels

- ✓ Fabric 3 quilter's cotton scraps for six 1" kites

- ✓ DMC floss - 989 (forest green), 369 (very light pistachio green), 335 (rose), 3354 (light dusty rose) 818 (baby pink), 3779 (ultra very light terracotta), 760 (salmon)

- ✓ Embroidery needle

- ✓ Water or heat erasable marker

- ✓ Pins or quilting clips

- ✓ Quilt basting spray

- ✓ 16" (40cm) square cushion insert

- ✓ Glue basting pen

- ✓ Light pad (optional)

- ✓ Cushion Cover template (and thick paper) or English paper piecing papers in the following quantities;

  • One 2" hexagon

  • Six 2" equilateral triangles

  • Twelve 1" jewels

  • Six 1" kites

- ✓ General sewing supplies

INSTRUCTIONS

1 If you do not have premade English paper piecing templates, use the templates included in the back of the book to trace and then precisely cut the required shapes from thick paper. See the section on English Paper Piecing Techniques at the beginning of the book for more tips on this process.

2 Glue baste six 2" equilateral triangles to Fabric 1, twelve 1" jewels to Fabric 2 and then six 1" kites to Fabric 3.

3 Centre a paper copy of the 2" hexagon floral embroidery design behind the 6" (15cm) square of pale cotton fabric. Trace the design with an erasable marker. Use a light pad, or press the paper template and fabric against a well-lit window, to help illuminate the design.

4 Place the fabric into the embroidery hoop so that it is taut.

5 Use the stitch types (indicated on the template) to embroider the floral design using two strands of DMC floss in the varying shades listed in the materials. The design includes flowers and leaves sewn in back stitch, lazy daisy stitch and French knots. For more details on the stitch types, see the Stitch Library. Sew the back stitch areas whilst the fabric is in the hoop. Remove the fabric from the hoop to sew the lazy daisy stitches and French knots (these particular stitches require the fabric to 'give' and so are best sewn out of the hoop).

6 Centre the embroidery design over a 2" paper hexagon template. Trim the fabric no less than ¼" (6mm) away from the edge of the template.

7 Glue baste the fabric to the hexagon paper.

8 Add the six triangles to the sides of the embroidered hexagon. Again, see the English Paper Piecing Techniques section for tips.

9 Add two jewels between each triangle so that their long points are facing in toward the embroidery.

10 Stitch the short sides of the kite shapes to the gap between the jewels. This will complete the design.

11 Carefully remove the paper templates from the back of the design, pressing as you go to help the panel keep its shape.

12 Roughly trace the panel onto the paper side of the fusible webbing. Cut out the webbing about 1/8" (3mm) inside the traced line. Iron the webbing onto the wrong side of the paper pieced panel. Make sure the outer seams of the panel remain folded under so there are no raw edges. Peel off the backing paper.

13 Position the panel over the centre of the 15" (38cm) square of fabric for the cushion front. Use a hot iron (and a press cloth) to secure the panel to the fabric.

14 For added durability, stitch the panel in place using a blind stitch to secure the turned fabric edges. See the Stitch Library for blind stitch tips.

15 Following the manufacturer's instructions, iron the square of fusible fleece to the wrong side of the cushion front.

16 Use the erasable marker and a ruler to mark a border no larger than ¼" (5mm) from the outside edge of the panel and the centre hexagon.

17 Hand quilt along this border using three strands of salmon DMC floss and a neat running stitch.

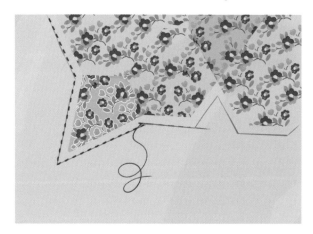

18 Use quilting basting spray to add an adhesive layer to the fusible fleece side of the cushion top. Position the square of backing fabric onto the fleece and press in place. You may also wish to baste stitch these three layers together using a ⅛" (3mm) seam allowance.

19 Make the envelope backing for the cushion by hemming the two 15" (38cm) x 11" (28cm) pieces of fabric. On the bottom of one fabric piece, fold the 15" (38cm) base up by 3/8" (1cm) and press, then fold over again and press. Use a straight stitch on the sewing machine to secure the hem in place. Repeat this process for the top of the other fabric piece.

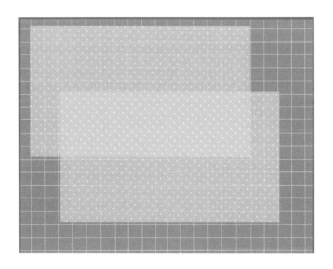

20 Place the cushion cover face down on a flat surface. Place the top hemmed fabric piece along the bottom of the cushion cover (right side facing out). Place the bottom hemmed fabric piece along the top of the cushion cover (also right side facing out). The hemmed edges will be overlapping in the centre. Pin or clip to the cushion front.

21 Sew the backing to the cushion cover front using a straight stitch and a scant ⅛" (3mm) seam allowance.

22 Ensure you have 70" (178") of continuous binding fabric that is 2" (5cm) wide, and folded over lengthways to make 1" (2.5cm) wide binding. Attach the binding to the front of the cushion using a ¼" (6mm) seam allowance. Be sure to carefully mitre each of the corners. (For more about the binding process, see the Patchwork and Quilting Techniques Section at the front of the book).

23 Press and fold the binding over to the back of the cushion cover and pin or clip in place. Then stitch the binding down using a single strand of matching thread and a blind stitch. The Stitch Library has more details on blind stitching.

24 Pop your cushion insert into the cover!

Ribbons and Bows Travel Clutch

The Ribbons and Bows Travel Clutch
is the perfect companion for all of your hair
accessories including clips, hair bands, combs and
ribbons. This folded clutch opens out to reveal top pockets,
a ribbon band, hanging loops and vinyl pockets on the base.
Great for travel and with terrific storage, this clutch keeps
all your pretties safely in one place. It features extra details
like a hexagon flower on the inside of the vinyl pocket and a
beautiful lazy daisy embroidery
detail on the outside.

Finished Size
Approximately 10" (25.5cm) wide
and 14" (35.5cm) tall (when laid flat) and 10"
(25.5cm) wide and 4 ¾" (12cm) when folded.

111

Materials

✓ 11" (28cm) x 15" (38cm) natural coloured linen for the outer

✓ Two 11" (28cm) x 15" (38cm) pieces of light weight fusible fleece

✓ 11" (28cm) x 15" (38cm) cotton floral fabric for the inner

✓ 53" (135cm) of cotton floral fabric bias cut binding

✓ 4 ½" (11.5cm) x 11" (28cm) clear vinyl

✓ 9" (23cm) x 11" (28cm) cotton floral fabric for the inner top pocket

✓ 4 ½" (11.5cm) x 11" (28cm) of light weight fusible interfacing

✓ 2" (5cm) x 14" (35.5cm) of heavy interfacing

✓ 1 ½" (3.8cm) square of scrap linen for a hexagon

✓ Six 1 ½" (3.8cm) squares of cotton floral fabric for the hexagons

✓ 22" (56cm) of picot edge bias binding in pale pink

✓ 3" (7.5cm) of ¾" (2cm) wide natural coloured cotton crochet lace

✓ 3" (7.5cm) of ¾" (2cm) wide natural coloured printed cotton tape

✓ 11" (28cm) of 1" (2.5cm) wide pale pink grosgrain ribbon

✓ 11" (28cm) of ½" (12mm) wide pale pink cotton crochet lace

✓ DMC floss in 760 (salmon), 818 (baby pink) and 369 (very light pistachio green)

✓ Water erasable pen

✓ Appliqué glue (optional)

✓ Small 2" (5cm) square of template plastic (optional)

✓ Matches, cigarette lighter or heat sealer (optional)

✓ Thick paper to create a template and hexagon shapes

✓ Thin tracing or tissue paper

✓ Glue basting pen for the hexagons

✓ 60 weight polyester bobbin thread in white

✓ Milliner's needle in size 9

✓ Rotary cutter, acrylic patchwork ruler and mat

✓ Quilting clips

✓ Small press stud

✓ Quilt basting (adhesive) spray

✓ Teflon sewing machine foot for sewing vinyl

✓ Ribbons and Bows Travel Clutch template

INSTRUCTIONS

NOTE: All seam allowances for this project are ¼" (6mm).

TIP: Use a walking foot on your sewing machine to complete this project. However, use a Teflon foot for the best results when sewing the vinyl pocket.

MAKE THE OUTER PANEL

1 Cut a paper rectangle measuring 10" (25.5cm) wide and 14" (35.5cm) tall. Fold the paper in half lengthways.

2 Trace the curved line of the top of the travel clutch template onto one end of the folded paper rectangle. Ensure the folded edge of the paper rectangle aligns with the side marked FOLD on the template, and that the top of the curve sits at the top of the paper. Cut along the traced line to make a large rectangular template with a curved top.

3 Follow the manufacturer's instructions to iron the fusible fleece to the wrong side of the 11" (28cm) x 15" (38cm) of linen.

4 Unfold the template and centre it on the right side of the linen and pin in place. Trace the outline of the template with a water erasable marker and remove the paper template. Keep the template for later.

5 Use a water erasable marker to draw cross-hatched quilting lines on the linen panel. Using the guides on a clear plastic patchwork ruler, draw a 45 degree diagonal line from the bottom left hand corner across to the other side. Measure 1 ½" (3.8cm) from the line and draw another parallel line. Continue to draw parallel diagonal lines the same distance apart to fill the linen shape.

6 Repeat the process to draw diagonally opposite lines from the bottom right hand corner. Continue until the linen shape is completely cross-hatched.

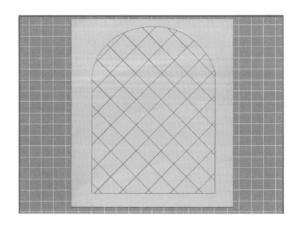

7 Sew along the marked lines using 60 weight polyester bobbin thread on your sewing machine.

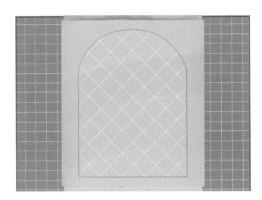

8 Remove the water erasable cross-hatched lines using a damp cloth. Be sure to keep the outer template lines intact though.

9 Use the ruler again to measure the centre of each cross-hatched square and mark it with a small dot.

10 Stitch a French knot over each centre dot using three strands and two loops of salmon DMC floss. The Stitch Library has more details on French Knots.

11 Use three strands of baby pink DMC floss to sew five lazy daisy stitches around each French knot, creating pink flowers. See the Stitch Library for more information on the Lazy Daisy Stitch.

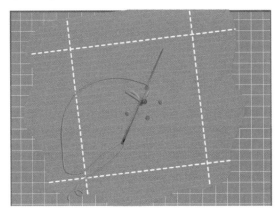

TIP: In order to ensure the flowers are uniformly stitched, you may wish to create a template by tracing the dots of the Petal Point Template onto template plastic. Heat the end of a pin with a match or lighter, and melt holes in the plastic that will be large enough to fit the erasable marker tip through. Place the template over each French knot and mark the five end points for the lazy daisy stitches. Then sew your perfectly arranged daisies on the linen.

12 Once all the daisies are stitched, remove the water erasable dots.

13 Press the linen, then cut out the linen shape on the template line. Set the linen panel aside.

MAKE THE INNER PANEL

14 Iron the second piece of fusible fleece to the wrong side of the 11" (28cm) x 15" (38cm) of inner floral fabric.

15 Pin the paper template to the centre of the floral fabric and trace around the outline using a water erasable marker. Remove the template.

16 Starting at the line on the base of the floral fabric, measure horizontal parallel lines at 1" (2.5cm) intervals and mark with an erasable marker.

17 Quilt along the lines using 60 weight polyester bobbin thread.

18 Use a damp cloth to remove the water erasable marker on the horizontal lines. Then press the fabric.

19 Cut out the fabric shape on the template line.

20 Iron the 2" (5cm) wide strip of heavy fusible interfacing to the centre back of this floral fabric panel. Use a press cloth or fabric scrap to protect the fusible fleece underneath.

21 Make the pocket for the top of the inner panel. Iron the 4 ½" (11.5cm) x 11" (28cm) of light weight fusible interfacing onto one half of the wrong side of the 9" (23cm) x 11" (28cm) of floral fabric for the pocket.

22 Fold the fabric in half along the top of the interfacing.

23 Cut the 22" (56cm) piece of picot edge binding in half. Use one half to bind the folded edge of the floral pocket. Open the binding on one side. Line up the raw edge of the binding with its right side facing down along the folded edge of the top of the pocket fabric. You may like to pin the binding in place. Stitch the binding in place along the first fold line.

24 Fold the binding over the folded fabric so that the picot edge of the binding is on the outside edge.

25 Top stitch the binding in place by sewing closely to the edge of the base of the binding. This will also secure the binding on the back of the fabric. This will become the top front pocket.

26 Pin this pocket onto the curved top of the inner panel with right side facing out. The long raw edge of the pocket should align with the curve at the top of the panel. The bound edge will become the opening for the pocket. Sew the pocket in place around the top curved edge of the fusible fleece, using a scant 1/8" (3mm) seam allowance. Then trim the corners of the pocket so that it matches the curved top of the panel.

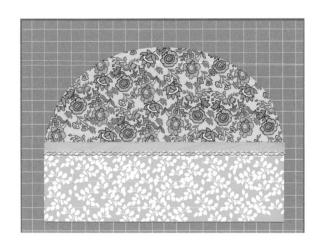

and cut seven ½" (12mm) hexagon templates onto heavy paper.

35 Use the hexagon papers to glue baste six hexagons, each using the 1 ½" (3.8cm) squares of floral fabric. These will form the petals of your hexagon flower. I 'fussy cut' the fabric so that there is a flower in the centre of each hexagon. For more detailed instructions on making and joining hexagons, see the English Paper Piecing Techniques section at the beginning of the book.

36 Use the same instructions in steps 10 and 11 to sew a lazy daisy to the centre of the 1 ½" (3.8cm) square of scrap linen. Then create a hexagon around this lazy daisy stitch by centring the hexagon paper over the flower, before trimming the linen and glue basting it to the hexagon paper.

37 Arrange the hexagons into a flower shape, and whip stitch the sides together using 60 weight bobbin thread and a milliner's needle.

38 Remove the backing papers and press.

27 Measure 5" (12.5cm) along the picot edge binding and draw a mark (this should be at the half way point). Use a water erasable marker to rule a vertical line up from this mark to divide the pocket into two equal sides. Sew along this line using a thread to match the pocket fabric. Be sure to back stitch at the beginning and end of your stitching, to firmly secure the pocket. Remove the erasable pen lines when complete. You now have two pockets at the top.

28 Make a decorative ribbon to attach hair clips to. Draw a line along the centre of the length of 1" (2.5cm) grosgrain ribbon.

29 Secure the 11" (28cm) cotton crochet lace to the centre of the ribbon (using the line as a guide). Use pins or a very small amount of appliqué glue to hold the lace over the ribbon centre.

30 Sew the lace to the ribbon along the top and base of the lace edges.

31 Position the ribbon at 1"- 2" (2.5cm - 5cm) below the inner panel pocket and pin in place. Use the quilted lines as a guide. Sew the ribbon using a scant 1/8" (3mm) seam allowance along both of the short ends at each side of the panel. Backstitch over the stitch lines for added durability.

32 Place a vertical line 5" (12.5cm) from the edge (or in the centre) of the ribbon. Sew along this line, then reverse over this line, to secure the centre of the ribbon to the panel. It should line up with the centre line of the top pocket.

33 Fold both of the 3" (7.5cm) pieces of lace and cotton tape in half. Pin the raw edges of the cotton tape along the raw edges of the panel (and over the ends of the ribbon) on the right hand side. Sew the cotton tape in place with a ⅛" (3mm) seam allowance. Use the same process to secure the lace tab to the left hand side of the panel at 1" (2.5cm) below the base of the ribbon. These tabs are great for bobby pins and slides.

34 Make a hexagon flower to decorate the base of the inner panel. Use the template to accurately trace

39 Position the hexagon flower on the bottom left of the inner panel approximately 1 ¼" (3.2cm) in from the left and bottom edges. Pin in place and then secure using a blind stitch.

40 Quilt closely around the outside of the hexagon flower using two strands of pistachio green DMC floss and a fine running stitch.

41 Make the vinyl pocket. Be sure to use a Teflon sewing machine foot. Use the same process used in steps 23 - 25 to secure the remaining piece of picot edge binding to the top of one side of the clear vinyl.

TIP: The vinyl may want to 'stick' to the sewing machine base. So before sewing, place a large piece of tracing or tissue paper under the vinyl and use it to help guide the vinyl through the machine. Simply sew straight through the paper and peel it away after stitching.

42 Top stitch the binding in place along the base of the binding. Again use tracing paper and your Teflon sewing machine foot.

43 Use the water erasable pen to place a mark on the inner fabric panel at the very centre of the base. Measure 4" (10cm) up vertically and place another very small mark.

44 Centre the vinyl pocket with the binding facing the top, on the base of the inner panel. Ensure the binding sits just above the fourth quilted line. You will need to trim the sides a little but still ensure there is a small overhang of vinyl on each of the three sides. Use quilting clips to hold the pocket in place (as pins will leave holes in the vinyl).

45 Use your Teflon foot to sew a vertical line down the centre of the vinyl pocket (using the small marks you just made as guides). Start just above the binding edge and sew down over the binding to the base of the inner panel. Remove the erasable marks by dampening them from the back of the panel.

46 Now sew the vinyl to the side and bottom edges of the inner panel using a scant ⅛" (3mm) seam allowance. Trim away any excess vinyl. You may wish to continue your seam up each side of the panel to the base of the top pocket, so that the whole panel is stitched around the perimeter.

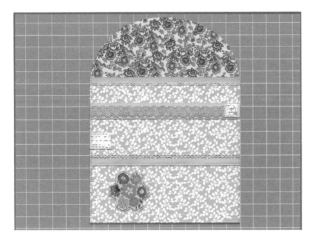

BIND THE PANELS TOGETHER

47 Press both panels with a warm iron on the wrong side in preparation for binding. Cover the panels with a press cloth and be careful to avoid placing the iron near the vinyl.

48 Spray the wrong side of both panels with quilt basting adhesive spray. Align the panels to fit together neatly and press them together with your hands. Set aside.

49 You will need 53" (135cm) of continuous bias binding that is 2" (5cm) wide. Cut enough fabric strips on the bias (on a 45 degree diagonal angle from the selvedge or fabric edge) to make the required length of binding. The binding needs to be bias cut so that the fabric can stretch around the top curved edge of the travel clutch. For more detailed instructions and extra tips on quilt binding, see the Patchwork and Quilting Techniques section at the beginning of the book.

50 Join the fabric strips on the diagonal. Remember to trim away the excess seam allowance and press the seams open.

51 Fold the fabric strip in half lengthways and press. Attach the binding to the top of the inner floral panel ensuring the raw edges of the binding line up with the raw edges of the panel. You will not need to use the Teflon foot on the vinyl pocket as the binding will cover the vinyl as you sew it in place. Use a ¼" (6mm) seam allowance. Be careful to mitre the bottom corners neatly, and join the binding ends neatly.

52 When finished, fold the binding over towards the linen outside of the travel clutch, carefully mitring the corners. Use quilting clips to hold the binding in place.

53 Using a single strand of 60 weight bobbin thread, blind stitch the binding to the linen outer panel with small, fine stitches. For more about blind stitching, see the Stitch Library.

54 Finish the travel clutch by adding a press stud. (Alternatively, you may wish to add a Velcro dot or a button and loop.) Sew one half of the press stud to the top of the top pocket on the inner panel (being careful that your stitches cannot be seen on the outside of the clutch).

55 Fold the clutch closed and use the water erasable pen to mark where to position the opposite press stud. It's useful to add a few accessories to the holder so that you can ensure everything fits when the holder is fastened closed.

56 Stitch the press stud in place, ensuring the stitches cannot be seen on the inside panel of the clutch.

Flower Friends Pincushions

Peach Petunia, Susie
Sunflower and Pink Peony are sure
to brighten up any sewing space, with their
glorious petals and sunny smiles. Make just one
or create a whole garden! Entirely hand stitched, they
make a great portable sewing project for travel. And
each of these pincushions can be sewn
in as little as an afternoon!

Finished Size
Approximately 3 ½" (9cm) across and
2" (5cm) high

Materials

✓ *Felt as outlined for each pincushion below*

✓ *DMC floss as outlined for each pincushion below*

✓ *Polyester hobby fill*

✓ *Handful of rice (or similar) to weigh down the pincushion*

✓ *Embroidery needle*

✓ *Freezer paper*

✓ *Paper backed fusible bonding web like Vliesofix*

✓ *Tissue paper*

✓ *Pen*

✓ *Pins*

✓ *Flower Friends Pincushion template*

PEACH PETUNIA

✓ *4" (10cm) square of peach wool felt for flower piece*

✓ *9 ½" (24cm) x 4 ½" (11.5cm) light green wool felt for pincushion top, base and side*

✓ *1.5" (4cm) x 1" (2.5cm) medium green wool felt for one leaf*

✓ *2" (5cm) x 1" (2.5cm) tan wool felt for hair*

✓ *2" (5cm) square of cream wool felt for face*

✓ *DMC floss in Ecru, 369 (very light pistachio green), 989 (forest green), 3790 (ultra dark beige gray), 352 (light coral), 353 (peach)*

SUSIE SUNFLOWER

✓ *3 ½" (9cm) x 7" (18cm) yellow wool felt for two flower pieces*

✓ *9 ½" (24cm) x 4 ½" (11.5cm) light green wool felt for pincushion top, base, side and one leaf*

✓ *1.5" (4cm) x 1" (2.5cm) medium green wool felt for one leaf*

✓ *2" (5cm) x 1" (2.5cm) tan wool felt for hair*

✓ *2" (5cm) square of cream wool felt for face*

✓ *DMC floss in Ecru, 369 (very light pistachio green), 3790 (ultra dark beige gray), 605 (very light cranberry)*

PINK PEONY

✓ *2 1/4" (6cm) square of pale pink felt for inner flower piece*

✓ *2 3/4" (7cm) square of dark pink felt for middle flower piece*

✓ *3 ½" (9cm) square of medium pink felt for outer flower piece*

✓ *9 ½" (24cm) x 4 ½" (11.5cm) medium green wool felt for pincushion top, base, side and one leaf*

✓ *1.5" (4cm) x 2" (5cm) light green wool felt for two leaves*

✓ *2" (5cm) x 1" (2.5cm) tan wool felt for hair*

✓ *2" (5cm) square of cream wool felt for face*

✓ *DMC floss in Ecru, 989 (medium green), 3790 (ultra dark beige gray), 605 (very light cranberry)*

INSTRUCTIONS

1 Trace the Flower Friends template pieces onto freezer paper and cut out.

2 Iron the freezer paper templates to the wool felt with a warm iron. Cut out the required felt shapes for each pincushion using the materials list as a guide. Each pincushion will need a base and top, a side, hair and face, petals, and leaves. Peel off the freezer paper.

3 Stitch the pincushion base. Using two strands of matching green DMC floss, blanket stitch the long side of the strip of felt to the outside edge of the circle base. Continue to stitch around the perimeter of the base until you reach your starting point. Overlap the felt of the side piece by ¼" (6mm). Trim away any excess felt if necessary.

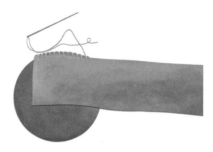

4 Blanket stitch the sides together, starting at the base and stitching to the top. Secure the stitching well and hide on the inside of the pincushion. Set the base aside.

5 Stitch the pincushion face. Position the piece of hair over the face and pin in place. With two strands of ultra dark beige gray DMC floss, and using a fine running stitch, sew the hair along the bottom of the hair line.

6 Trace the head shape and facial details onto a small piece of tissue paper and cut around the outside edge of the face shape.

7 Pin the paper over the felt face, making sure the hair line matches up with the traced details. Using two strands of ultra dark beige gray DMC floss, back stitch the eyes by sewing directly through the paper. Stitch the length of one eye first, then the eye lashes. Then stitch the next eye and lashes. Stitch the mouth with two strands of very light cranberry (or peach for Peach Petunia).

8 When you've finished stitching, hold the stitches with one hand as you gently tear away the paper with the other. Tease any stray pieces of paper out from under the stitches with your needle (if necessary).

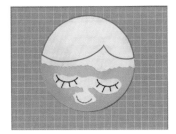

9 Attach the completed face to the petals and the pincushion top.

FOR PEACH PETUNIA

- For extra detail, blanket stitch the outside edge of all the petals of the peach flower felt using two strands of peach DMC floss.
- Centre the flower petal piece over the middle of the pincushion top and secure with a few stitches.
- Attach the face to the centre top of the flower petal piece using fusible web.
- Blanket stitch the outside edge of the face using two strands of DMC floss (changing colours for face and hair). Be sure to stitch through all the felt layers including the pincushion top.
- Blanket stitch the outside edge of one medium green felt leaf using two strands of forest green DMC floss. Use a few stitches to secure the leaf to the pincushion top (under the petals).

FOR SUNFLOWER SUSIE

- Overlap the two sunflower petal pieces so that the petals are evenly spaced. Secure with a few stitches.
- Centre the flower petal piece over the middle of the pincushion top and again secure with a few stitches.
- Attach the face to the centre top of the sunflower petal piece using fusible web.
- Blanket stitch the outside edge of the face using two strands of DMC floss (changing colours for face and hair). Be sure to stitch through all the felt layers including the pincushion top.
- Secure one medium green leaf and one light green leaf to the pincushion top by stitching them in place using a few small stitches under the petals.

FOR PINK PEONY

- Overlap the three layers of petal pieces so that the petals are evenly spaced. Secure with a few stitches.
- Centre the flower petal piece over the middle of the pincushion top and again secure with a few stitches.
- Attach the face to the centre top of the sunflower petal piece using fusible web.
- Blanket stitch the outside edge of the face using two strands of DMC floss (changing colours for face and hair). Be sure to stitch through all the felt layers including the pincushion top.
- Secure one medium green leaf and two light green leaves to the pincushion top, by stitching them in place using a few small stitches under the petals.

10 Place your completed pincushion top over the pincushion base. Pin in place, making sure to position the side seam (of the base) at the centre back of the head.

11 Starting at the side seam, blanket stitch the pincushion top to the sides using two strands of matching DMC floss. Stitch three quarters of the way around the top and leave a small gap for stuffing. Insert a layer of rice into the open gap; enough to cover the base of the pincushion, and firmly stuff the pincushion with hobby fill. Continue to blanket stitch the pincushion closed.

TIP: As an alternative to hobby fill and rice, fill your pincushion with ground walnut shells to give it weight and keep your pins sharp.

DIFFICULTY LEVEL
INTERMEDIATE

Strawberry Surprise Journal Cover

There's something so deliciously
'summery' about strawberries. They look so
pretty adorning this beautiful A5 diary cover. With
hand embroidery, appliqué, felt work, and binding, this
project covers a whole range of techniques. It is the extra
details that make this project special though, including the
simple pocket inside the front cover, the felt strawberry
on the back cover and the ribbon detail.
Your diary or planner never
looked so good!

Finished Size
Approximately 7 ¼" (18.5cm) wide and 10"
(25.5cm) tall

123

Materials

✓ Two rectangles 14" (37cm) x 10" (25.5cm) of linen fabric for cover

✓ 24" (61cm) by 10" (25.5cm) of fabric A for diary cover sleeves

✓ 6" (15cm) x 8" (20cm) of fabric B for pocket

✓ 6" (15cm) x width of fabric for the binding fabric

✓ 6" (15cm) square of white quilter's cotton fabric for the embroidered patch

✓ 16" (41cm) x 10" (25.5cm) of light weight fusible interfacing

✓ 14" (35.5cm) x 10" (25.5cm) of fusible fleece or wadding like Pellon Vilene

✓ Small scraps of paper backed fusible appliqué bonding web like Vliesofix

✓ 100% wool felt scraps in strawberry red, dark green, white and yellow

✓ DMC floss in 702 (kelly green), 772 (very light yellow green), B5200 (snow white), 445 (light lemon), 3801 (very dark melon), 602 (medium cranberry)

✓ Two 12" (30.5cm) lengths of ⅜" (1cm) wide grosgrain ribbon (pink and green)

✓ 60 weight polyester bobbin thread in white

✓ Embroidery needle

✓ 4" (10cm) timber embroidery hoop

✓ 4" (10cm) x 1" (2.5cm) rectangle of light cardboard

✓ Sewing pins or quilting clips

✓ Quilt basting (adhesive) spray

✓ Water erasable marking pen

✓ A5 - 5.8" x 8.3" (148mm x 210mm) soft cover spiral bound notebook

✓ Rotary cutter, ruler and cutting mat

✓ Light pad (optional)

✓ Strawberry Surprise Journal template

INSTRUCTIONS

MAKE THE EMBROIDERED DIARY LABEL

1 Trace the word 'Diary' from the template on the centre of the white quilter's cotton. Illuminate the template with a light pad or press the template and fabric up to a well-lit window. Complete the tracing with a water erasable marker.

2 Place the white cotton firmly in an embroidery hoop, and back stitch the text with three strands of medium cranberry DMC floss. Remove from the hoop, dampen the fabric to remove the erasable marker and then press.

3 Mark a 5" (12.5cm) x 2" (5cm) box around the centre of the design, using a ruler and erasable marker. Cut out the design.

4 Centre the front of the 'Diary' fabric over the 4" (10cm) x 1" (2.5cm) rectangle of light cardboard. Turn over and press the fabric edges over the card. Using a single strand of 60 weight polyester thread, baste stitch the folded edges down (being sure not to sew through the cardboard.

5 Gently pop the cardboard out of the fabric. Press the label flat.

6 Press a 4" (10cm) x 1" (2.5cm) rectangle of paper backed fusible web to the back of the Diary label. Peel off the paper backing.

7 Fold one piece of linen fabric in half with the fold line to the left like a book. This will be the outside of the journal cover. Position the Diary label about 2 ½" (6.5cm) down from the top edge of the fabric, and 1 ½" (4cm) in from the left hand fold. Press the label in place with a warm iron.

8 Use a single strand of white 60 weight polyester thread to blind stitch the edges of the Diary label to the linen.

9 Using the water erasable marker and ruler, draw a rectangular border ⅛" (3mm) in from the Diary label edge.

10 Using three strands of very light yellow green DMC floss, sew a short fine running stitch along this line.

11 Mark a small dot in the top right and bottom left corners of the label (just in from the stitched border). Using two strands of DMC floss and a lazy daisy stitch, sew a very dark melon red flower on the bottom left and a lemon flower on the top right of the label.

12 Erase the lines and marks with a damp cloth when the embroidery is complete.

EMBROIDER THE STRAWBERRY DETAIL

13 Use a light pad or a bright window to trace the strawberry embroidery design onto the front of the linen cover (centred below the diary label). Use the water erasable marker to draw all details except the dots indicating French knots on the large strawberry and flower shape.

14 Trace the large strawberry and strawberry top appliqué shapes, the small strawberry shapes, and the flower shape and flower centre onto paper backed fusible web. (Note that these templates are already reversed for appliqué.) Roughly cut around each template piece and then iron each onto the corresponding felt colours; the strawberry on red, strawberry top on green, flower on white and flower centre on lemon. Cut each felt piece on the template line then remove the backing paper.

15 Position the large strawberry and flower on the traced embroidery design. (Put the small strawberry aside for now). The strawberry top goes over the strawberry shape and the lemon flower circle is centred over the white flower shape. Secure the felt in place with a warm iron.

16 Appliqué the felt shapes in place using two strands of the coordinating coloured DMC floss. Blanket stitch around the red strawberry shape and the white flower. Blanket stitch around the lemon flower centre. Use fine small running stitches in Kelly green to secure the strawberry top. Use the water erasable marker (and the template as a guide) to mark in the dots for the French knots. With two strands of DMC floss, sew white French knots for the strawberry seeds and lemon knots around the flower centre.

17 Continue to embroider the remaining details on the linen. Use two strands of DMC floss for all stitches. The strawberry leaves are back stitched in kelly green. The swirls are back stitched in very light yellow green. The lazy daisy flowers are sewn in white with lemon French knot centres.

18 When all the embroidery is complete, carefully erase the template lines with water.

19 Position the small felt strawberry on the opposite side of the linen cover about 1" (2.5cm) in from the bottom left corner. (This will appear on the back cover). Overlap the strawberry top on the strawberry shape. Press in place with a warm iron. Use the same strawberry coloured floss to blanket stitch the strawberry shape, and running stitch the strawberry top.

ASSEMBLE THE DIARY COVER

20 Press the journal cover. Follow the manufacturer's instructions to secure the rectangle of fusible fleece to the wrong side of the other rectangle of linen (the journal lining). Spray the fleece side of the lining with quilt basting spray. Align the wrong side of the journal cover linen over the fleece and press together with your hands. The fleece will be sandwiched between both pieces of linen. Sew the linen together with a scant 1/8" (3mm) seam allowance around the outside edge.

21 Cut two rectangles of fabric A measuring 12" wide (30.5cm) by 10" (25.5cm) high. Fold in half and press. Cut two rectangles of fusible interfacing 6" (15cm) by 10" (25.5cm). Follow the manufacturer's instructions to iron the interfacing onto one half of each fabric rectangle. Then fold the other side of the fabric over. You'll now have two matching rectangles that will form the sleeves to hold the A5 journal in place.

22 Bind the open 10" (25.5cm) length of one fabric rectangle, using a 10" (25.5cm) strip of 2" wide binding fabric. Press the fabric strip in half lengthways. Pin the open edges of the fabric strip along the left hand edge of the fabric rectangle and stitch in place with a ¼" (6mm) seam allowance.

23 Fold the fabric strip over the edge of the rectangle and press down on the other side.

24 Pin or clip the fabric in place then blind stitch the binding down (being careful not to stitch through to the front of the fabric rectangle). Use a single strand of matching sewing thread. The right hand sleeve is complete.

25 To make a pocket for the left hand sleeve, cut a fabric rectangle 6" (15cm) wide and 8" (20cm) high. Press in half and secure a piece of 6" (15cm) x 4" (10cm) fusible interfacing to one half. Fold the fabric over.

26 Place the pocket against the base of the sleeve fabric, all raw edges aligned and the fold along the top, and pin in place. Using the method described previously, bind the right hand side of the fabric sleeve with 10" (25.5cm) of 2" (5cm) wide binding fabric pressed in half.

27 Pin or clip the sleeves to the edges of the linen cover. Stitch the sleeves in place around the entire outside edge of the linen cover, with a scant ⅛" (3mm) seam allowance. Be sure that the direction of the cover matches the direction of the lower left pocket.

28 Measure the top of the cover and mark the centre point. Baste stitch the two 12" (30.5cm) lengths of ribbon over the centre point.

BIND THE OUTSIDE EDGE OF THE DIARY COVER

29 Ensure you have 60" (152.5cm) of continuous binding fabric that is 2" (5cm) wide, and folded over lengthways to make 1" (2.5cm) wide binding. Attach the binding to the outside of the diary cover using a ¼" (6mm) seam allowance. Be sure to carefully mitre each of the corners. Pin the ribbons down and sew the binding over the top of them. (For more about the binding process, see the Quilting Techniques section at the front of the book).

30 Fold the binding over to the inside of the diary cover and pin or clip in place. Then stitch the binding down using a single strand of matching thread and a blind stitch.

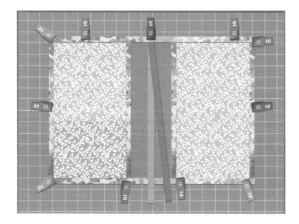

31 All that's left is to trim and heat seal the end of the one of the ribbons, and then sew a sweet strawberry charm to the end of the other. Use the small strawberry appliqué template and freezer paper to cut two green felt strawberry tops and two red strawberry shapes. Arrange the strawberries so that they are a mirror image of one another (and will match up when placed back to back). Sew the base of the green tops where they overlap the red

strawberries, using a very fine running stitch. Use a single strand of kelly green DMC floss.

32 Place the strawberries back-to-back and pin or clip together. With two strands of very dark melon DMC floss, blanket stitch the red strawberry shapes together (keeping the green top open).

33 Slide the end of the ribbon into the opening at the top of the strawberry. Pin in place. Continue to running stitch around the green strawberry top, but this time be sure to sew both green tops together. You will need to sew through the ribbon to hold the strawberry in place.

34 Slide the covers of an A5 sized diary into the cover sleeves. Use the ribbons to bookmark your favourite pages and keep notes and pens in the pocket on the left.

NOTE: This project includes many hand embroidery stitches. You can read more about each stitch type in the Stitch Library.

Please consult the Techniques section for further details about embroidery (in the Stitch Library), Appliqué Techniques, Working With Felt, and Quilting Techniques.

TIP: For best results, use a walking foot on your sewing machine. This quilting foot helps keep the fabric from stretching or moving as you sew.

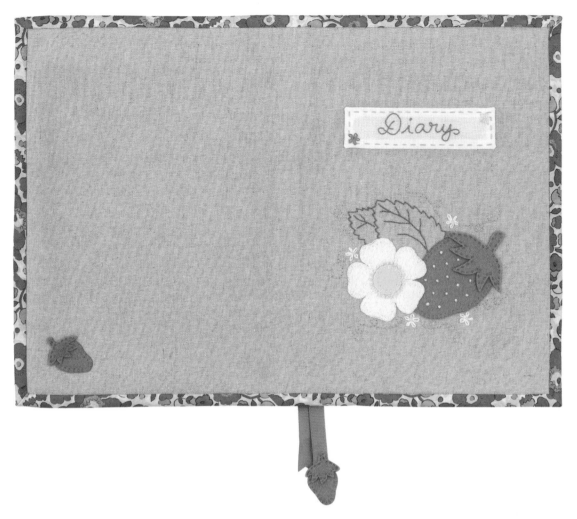

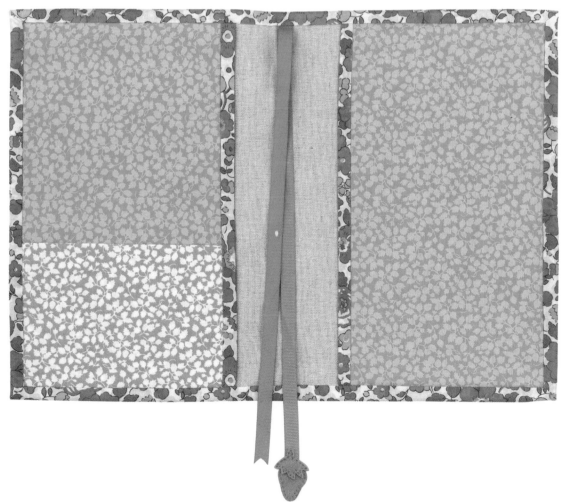

THE WIND

I saw you toss the kites on high
And blow the birds about the sky;
And all around I heard you pass,
Like ladies' skirts across the grass—
O wind, a-blowing all day long,
O wind, that sings so loud a song!

e and there,
ray,
air,
day;

winds that pass
e showers,
e meadow grass
ow flowers.

47

Strawberry Surprise Bookmark

*Made to match the Strawberry Surprise
Journal Cover, this bright and flowery bookmark is a quick
and easy make and it's a gorgeous way to brighten up any book!
The strawberry and flower are hand stitched in felt
and can be attached to fabric or ribbon.
Pair it with your diary or gift it to a
book-loving friend.*

Finished Size
Approximately 2" (5cm) wide x 13 ¾" (35cm)

Materials

✔ *Two 2" (5cm) x 11" (28cm) strips of floral fabric*

✔ *Two 1" (2.5cm) x 11" (28cm) strips of light weight fusible interfacing*

✔ *Wool felt scraps in strawberry red, dark green, white and yellow*

✔ *DMC floss in 702 (kelly green), B5200 (snow white), 445 (light lemon), 3801(very dark melon)*

✔ *Embroidery needle*

✔ *Pins or quilting clips*

✔ *Water erasable pen*

✔ *Freezer paper*

✔ *Strawberry Surprise Bookmark template*

INSTRUCTIONS

1 Cut the fabric strips for the bookmark. Iron the strips of fusible interfacing to the centre of the wrong side of the fabric strips (adhering to the manufacturer's instructions).

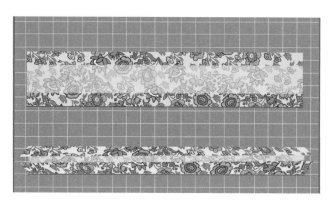

2 Fold the raw edges of each fabric strip over the interfacing and towards the centre of the fabric and press.

3 Place both strips of fabric together with right sides facing out and pin. Sew a small straight stitch down the length of each side using a scant ⅛" (3mm) seam allowance.

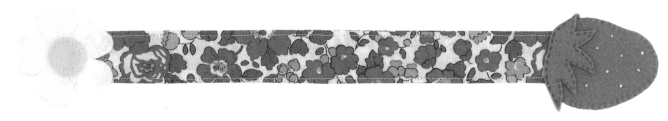

4 Trace the template shapes onto the paper side of the freezer paper and roughly cut out. Iron the shiny side of the freezer paper onto the felt and carefully cut out each felt piece as listed on the template. Peel off the freezer paper.

5 Lay the two white flower shapes out and ensure that they are a mirror image of one another. Pin one yellow flower circle over the centre of one flower shape. Blanket stitch it in place using two strands of lemon floss. Repeat for the other flower.

6 Place both flower shapes over the end of the fabric strip so that the strip reaches the centre of the flower. Match up the petals and pin in place. Secure the flower to the fabric with a fine running stitch using two strands of white DMC floss. Be sure to catch both sides of felt as you stitch through the petals and the fabric strip. Continue to stitch around the outside of every petal in the whole flower shape.

7 Lay the two strawberry shapes out and ensure that they are a mirror image of one another. Do the same with the strawberry tops.

47

8 With two strands of Kelly green DMC floss and using a fine running stitch, secure one strawberry top to a strawberry shape. Stitch along the leaves from one side of the strawberry to the other. Set aside and repeat for the other strawberry (ensuring that the length of the finished strawberries will match up when placed back to back).

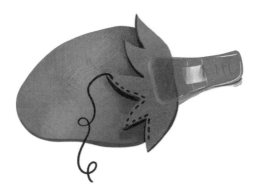

9 Using the template as a guide, mark the white French knots on the strawberry shapes using an erasable marker.

10 Stitch the French knots using two strands of white DMC floss.

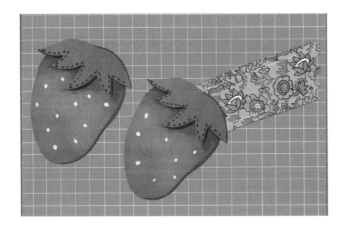

11 Use pins or quilting clips to hold the strawberries together with wrong sides facing. Blanket stitch the red strawberry shapes together with two strands of very dark melon DMC floss.

12 Insert the fabric strip no more than ½" (or about 1cm) into the opening of the strawberry at the top. Pin in place.

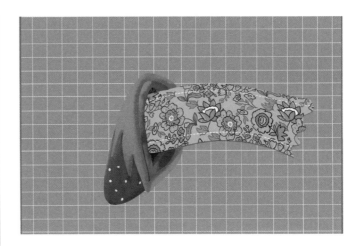

13 Now it's time to finish the strawberry top with running stitch, using the kelly green DMC floss. Start on one side of the strawberry to sew the strawberry tops together making sure you stitch through both layers of felt and the fabric. Be sure to keep your stitching even as you sew from one side of the strawberry, through the fabric, and to the other. When your stitching is complete, secure your floss with some extra stitches hidden inside the two felt layers. When finished, your stitching will look like one continuous running stitch around the whole outside edge of the strawberry top. Your bookmark is now complete.

TIP: Change the fabric length to suit your needs. Make it shorter for a novel, or longer for a scrapbook.

:here,

that pass

vers,

ow grass

wers.

Blossom Scissor Charm

Never lose your scissors in the sewing
room with this beautifully designed charm. Entirely hand
stitched in felt, this scissor decoration is simply adorable.
It also makes a fun and fresh bag charm. Instructions are
included to transform this lovely bloom into a pretty brooch
and a hair accessory too.

Finished Size
Approximate size of individual
flower 3" (7.5cm) across and
1" (2.5cm) high

Materials

- ✓ *Wool felt in green, pale pink, medium pink and lemon*
- ✓ *DMC floss in 369 (very light pistachio green)*
- ✓ *Embroidery needle*
- ✓ *Freezer paper*
- ✓ *Pins*
- ✓ *Felt cutting scissors*
- ✓ *Blossom Felt Flowers template*
- ✓ *8" (20cm) of narrow ⅜" (3mm) wide pink grosgrain ribbon (optional – for scissor charm)*
- ✓ *Brooch clasp (optional for brooch)*
- ✓ *48mm double pronged alligator clip (optional for hair accessory)*
- ✓ *4 ¾" (12cm) of ⅜" (1cm) wide grosgrain ribbon (optional for hair accessory)*
- ✓ *Glue gun (optional for hair accessory)*
- ✓ *Heat sealer or cigarette lighter to seal ribbon ends (optional)*

INSTRUCTIONS

1 Trace the Blossom flower template pieces onto freezer paper and cut out.

2 Iron the freezer paper templates to the wool felt with a warm iron. Cut out each template as listed below and then peel off the freezer paper.

-One leaf template shape in green (choose one of the two designs)

-One leaf centre template in green

-Two flower templates in different shades of the same felt colour. Be sure to cut out the centre holes of the flowers too.

3 To cut out the felt for the rolled centre (which fits inside the central hole in the petals), iron the template to the felt then cut out around the outside of the shape. Fold the template in half lengthways and cut the felt on the fold, following the template lines.

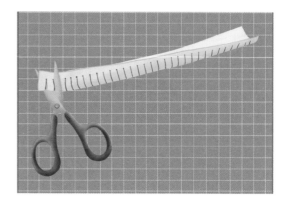

4 Peel off the freezer paper.

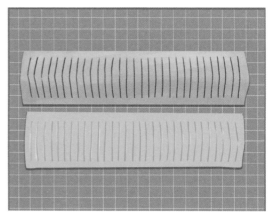

TIP: The freezer paper templates can be reused a number of times, so be sure to store them carefully.

5 Fold the rolled centre felt in half lengthways and then carefully roll up. Using a matching sewing thread, secure the rolled felt with small whip stitches around the base (opposite end to the felt loops). See the Stitch Library for more stitch details.

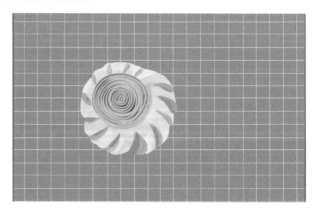

6 Overlap the two flower shapes so that the paler felt is on top (and the darker petals can be seen behind the paler petals above).

7 Place the base of the rolled felt through the centre of the flowers and secure with stitches.

8 Place the green leaf shape over the centre of the flower base. Stitch in place with two strands of very light pistachio green DMC floss and a simple whip stitch. Sew through the bottom layer of felt petals only.

Follow the remaining steps to finish your felt flower as a scissor charm, brooch or hair accessory.

TO MAKE A SCISSOR CHARM

1 Fold an 8" (20cm) length of narrow 1/8" (3mm) wide grosgrain ribbon in half to make a loop. Secure the ends of the ribbon to the centre of the green leaf circle using a few small stitches.

2 Cover the centre of the leaf template with the circle of green leaf-centre felt. Blanket stitch it in place with two strands of very light pistachio green DMC floss.

3 Push the ribbon loop through one scissor handle.

4 Carefully manoeuvre the felt flower through the ribbon loop and pull gently. Your scissor charm is complete.

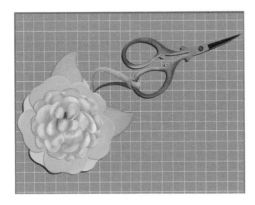

TO MAKE A BROOCH

1 Using small, fine stitches, sew a brooch clasp to the leaf centre circle of felt.

2 Pin or clip the circle of felt to the back of the flower and blanket stitch it in place using two strands of green DMC floss.

3 Attach your pretty brooch to a cardigan, or even your favourite bag.

TO MAKE A HAIR ACCESSORY

1 Use your heat sealer to seal the ends of the 4 ¾" (12cm) of grosgrain ribbon. Alternatively, run the flame from a cigarette lighter across the end of the ribbon to melt the fibres and seal the ends.

2 Set up your glue gun and allow it time to heat up.

3 Open the alligator clip and run some hot glue along the underside of the top 'jaw' of the clip. Slide your ribbon into the open space between the jaws and attach it to the glue.

4 With your clip facing up, run a length of hot glue across the top of the clip right to the end of the jaw. Fold your ribbon back over the top and gently smooth it across the top jaw using your thumb.

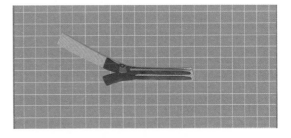

5 Place a small dab of hot glue on both ends of the inside of the jaws at the back. Be careful not to get any glue near the spring though, or you'll have a clip that won't close properly. Gently push the ribbon into the space at the back.

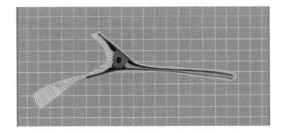

6 Lastly put a small dollop of hot glue on the underside of the clip, before the start of the prongs. Fold the remaining length of ribbon over and press down to secure.

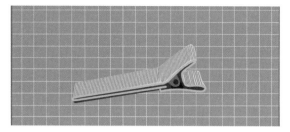

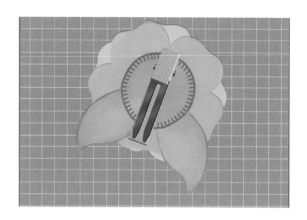

7 Run a length of hot glue along the top of the covered clip. Secure the clip to the back of the felt flower over the green felt centre.

8 The pretty felt clip is all ready for use!

Lovely Leaf Scissor Keeper

Hand stitch this felt leaf to securely store your delicate
embroidery scissors. Simply tuck them into the opening on
the front. Add a 'Blossom Scissor Charm' to the handle on
your scissors and then team your lovely leaf with one of the pretty
'Flower Friends' pincushions.
Bring Spring to your sewing room!

Finished Size
Approximately 4 ¾" (12 cm) long and 3 ½" (9 cm) wide
To fit embroidery scissors measuring approximately 3 ½" (9 cm) long and
1 ¾" (4.5 cm) wide

Materials

- ✓ Three 5" (13cm) x 3 ¾" (9.5cm) pieces of medium green wool felt

- ✓ Two 5" (13cm) x 3 ¾" (9.5cm) pieces of light weight fusible interfacing

- ✓ DMC floss 989 (forest green), 369 (very light pistachio green)

- ✓ Embroidery needle

- ✓ Freezer paper

- ✓ Tissue paper

- ✓ Pen

- ✓ Pins

- ✓ Lovely Leaf Scissor Keeper template

INSTRUCTIONS

1 Following the manufacturer's instructions, iron the fusible interfacing to one side of two (of the three pieces) of wool felt.

2 Copy or trace the three Lovely Leaf Scissor Keeper template pieces onto the paper side of the freezer paper and roughly cut around each shape.

3 Iron the freezer paper templates to the wool felt with a warm iron. Be sure to iron the 'leaf base' and the 'leaf top' to the front of the two pieces of felt lined with interfacing. Iron the 'leaf middle' template to the plain piece of wool felt.

4 Cut out each leaf shape following the template outline and peel off the freezer paper. Don't forget to carefully cut along the 'scissor opening' line as indicated on the template for the leaf top.

5 Blanket stitch around the scissor opening of the leaf top piece using two strands of forest green DMC floss. This will seal the raw edges of the felt and protect it from stretching. Your scissors will move in and out of this opening.

6 Add the leaf vein details to the front of the leaf top piece using two strands of very light pistachio green DMC floss.

Trace the leaf template shape and the vein details onto tissue paper. Don't forget to also mark the scissor opening, as you don't want to stitch through it! Cut around the outside of the tissue paper and pin the paper over the top leaf piece. Back stitch the leaf vein details onto the felt, by sewing through the paper template. As you sew the leaf spine, stop when you reach the opening in the felt for the scissors. Finish off your stitching on the interfaced (back) side of the felt. Knot your thread again and resume sewing the spine detail on the opposite side of the opening. Make sure you do not accidentally stitch the opening closed.

7 When you've finished stitching, hold the stitches with one hand as you gently tear away the paper with the other. Tease any stray pieces of paper out from under the stitches with your needle (if necessary).

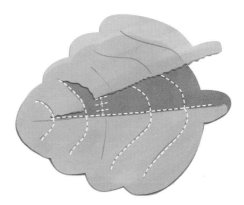

8 Sandwich the leaf middle piece between the two outer leaf shapes. Note that this piece is slightly smaller than the top and base. Ensuring that the interfacing of the leaf top and leaf bottom are facing the leaf middle and cannot be seen from the outside, pin all three layers of felt together.

9 Blanket stitch around the outside edge of the leaf with two strands of forest green DMC floss. This will secure all three layers of felt together.

10 When finished, pop your scissors into the opening of the leaf, ensuring the tip of the blades fit neatly inside the leaf stem.

TIP: Adorn your scissor keeper with some felt flowers using felt flowers from Polly Plait's flower crown.

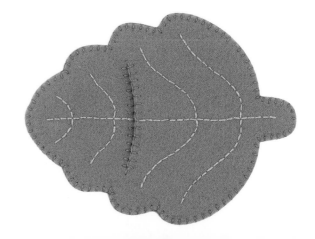

Garden Path Mini Quilt

Meander up the garden path with pretty florals arranged in a rainbow of blooms. You'll love this project if you're just starting your journey into hand sewing hexagons and hand quilting too. Finish off this lovely piece on the sewing machine and you're all set to decorate your sewing space, or gift it to a creative friend or green thumb.

Finished Size
14 ½" (37cm) long and 12 3/4" (32.5cm) high

141

Materials

- ✓ 35 x 2 ½" (6cm) squares of different coordinating fabrics
- ✓ 4" (10cm) x width of fabric for binding
- ✓ 14" (35.5cm) x width of fabric of natural coloured linen
- ✓ 11" (28cm) x 10" (25.5cm) light weight fusible interfacing
- ✓ 15 ½" (39.5cm) x 13 ½" (34.5cm) fusible fleece
- ✓ DMC floss in 335 (rose)
- ✓ Water erasable pen
- ✓ Hexie mini quilt template and thick paper to create hexagon shapes
- ✓ Glue basting pen
- ✓ 60 weight polyester bobbin thread in white, grey or beige
- ✓ Milliner's needle in size 9
- ✓ Rotary cutter, ruler and mat
- ✓ Quilt basting (adhesive) spray
- ✓ General sewing supplies

INSTRUCTIONS

NOTE: All seam allowances for this project are ¼" (6mm).

TIP: This project is best stitched with a walking foot on your sewing machine.

MAKE THE HEXAGON PANEL

1 Use the template provided to trace and cut 35 identical 1" paper hexagon shapes. Use each hexagon paper to glue-baste 35 hexagons, each with a different 2 ½" (6cm) fabric square. For more detailed instructions on making and sewing hexagons, see the English Paper Piecing Techniques at the beginning of the book.

2 Arrange the hexagons in a panel (seven across and five high) so that the flat sides are facing the top and bottom. There will be a point on the left and right sides of the hexagons. My hexagons are roughly arranged from lightest in the top left corner to darkest in the bottom right corner. When you are happy with the layout, photograph your panel so that you can refer to the image as you stitch.

3 Hand sew the hexagon panel together with whip stitch, using fine polyester bobbin thread and a size 9 milliner's needle.

4 Remove the papers from the back of the hexagon panel, starting with those in the centre. Press the panel as you go, to help keep the hexagons in shape.

5 Line the back of the hexagon panel with light weight fusible interfacing. Cut the interfacing to match the shape of the panel before securing it to the panel back with a warm iron.

6 Using a rotary cutter and ruler, trim the hexagon panel down to 9 ½" (24cm) long and 8" (20cm) high. Make sure the panel remains centred and the hexagon seams remain straight.

ASSEMBLE THE QUILT

7 Cut the linen pieces for the hexagon border. You will need two strips measuring 9 ½" (24cm) long and 3" (7.5cm) high. You will also need two strips measuring 3" (7.5cm) wide and 12 3/4" (32.5cm) high.

8 With right sides facing, pin and sew one 9 ½" (24cm) strip of linen to the top of the hexagon panel. Repeat this process with the second piece of linen and sew it to the base of the hexagon panel. Press the seams toward the linen fabric.

9 With right sides facing, pin and sew the 12 ¾" (32.5cm) strip of linen to the left of the quilt panel. Repeat this for the right side of the panel. Press the seams toward the linen fabric.

10 Cut a panel of linen 15 ½" (39.5cm) long x 13 ½" (34.5cm) high for the quilt backing. Secure the fusible fleece to the wrong side (following the manufacturer's instructions).

11 Spray the fleece side of the linen quilt backing with quilt basting spray and centre the hexagon quilt panel over the top of the base. Press with your hands to fuse the two layers together and remove any lumps or bumps. The backing will be larger than the top and will be trimmed to size after quilting.

12 Mark diagonal lines on the quilt top using a water erasable pen. Draw a line from the top left corner across to the bottom right corner. Mark lines on either side of this central line at 1" (2.5cm) intervals. Continue until the quilt top is completely marked with diagonal lines.

Repeat this process by drawing a diagonal line from the top right corner of the quilt top, to the bottom left corner. Again draw lines at 1" (2.5cm) intervals on either side of this central line until the entire quilt top is marked with diamond shaped lines.

13 Thread your sewing machine with 60 weight polyester thread and sew over these lines to quilt the layers of the hexie quilt together. Start sewing the lines in the centre of the quilt and work your way outwards, to help avoid any puckering. Continue sewing until all the quilting is completed.

14 It's now time to add a small border of hand quilting around the hexagon panel. Using a ruler and a water soluble marker, draw a border on the linen fabric ¼" (6mm) from the hexagon panel.

Hand embroider the bow detail with back stitch, using three strands of rose DMC floss. Also use three strands of floss to quilt the border using running stitch. For more details on back stitch and running stitch, please see the Stitch Library.

Dampen the lines on the quilt to remove the water erasable pen marks before you press the quilt flat.

15 Using a rotary cutter and ruler, trim the edges of the quilt so that it measures 14 ½" (37cm) long and 12 3/4" (32.5cm) high. Keep the quilt square and ensure the sides are at right angles with the top and the bottom.

16 Bind the quilt with the binding fabric. Cut two strips of fabric 2" (5cm) wide and join them to create a continuous length of binding 65" (165cm) long. For more detailed instructions and extra tips on quilt binding, see the Patchwork and Quilting section at the beginning of the book. Fold the fabric strip in half lengthways and press. Attach the binding to the front of the quilt ensuring the raw edges of the binding line up with the raw edges of the quilt. Sew in place with a ¼" (6mm) seam allowance. Be careful to mitre the corners neatly, and join the binding ends neatly also.

17 When finished, fold the binding over towards the back of the quilt. Using a single strand of polyester bobbin thread, blind stitch the binding to the back of the quilt with small, fine stitches. For more detail about blind stitching, see the Stitch Library.

TEMPLATES

All templates in this book are in real size.

centre top

**Hoppy Squares
Table Tidy
Page 98**

ear shapes

inner
ear

inner
ear

folded
ear

face

FOLD

reversed for
appliqué

neck

collar

body shape

FOLD

TOP

Lullaby Kitty Felt Doll
Page 54

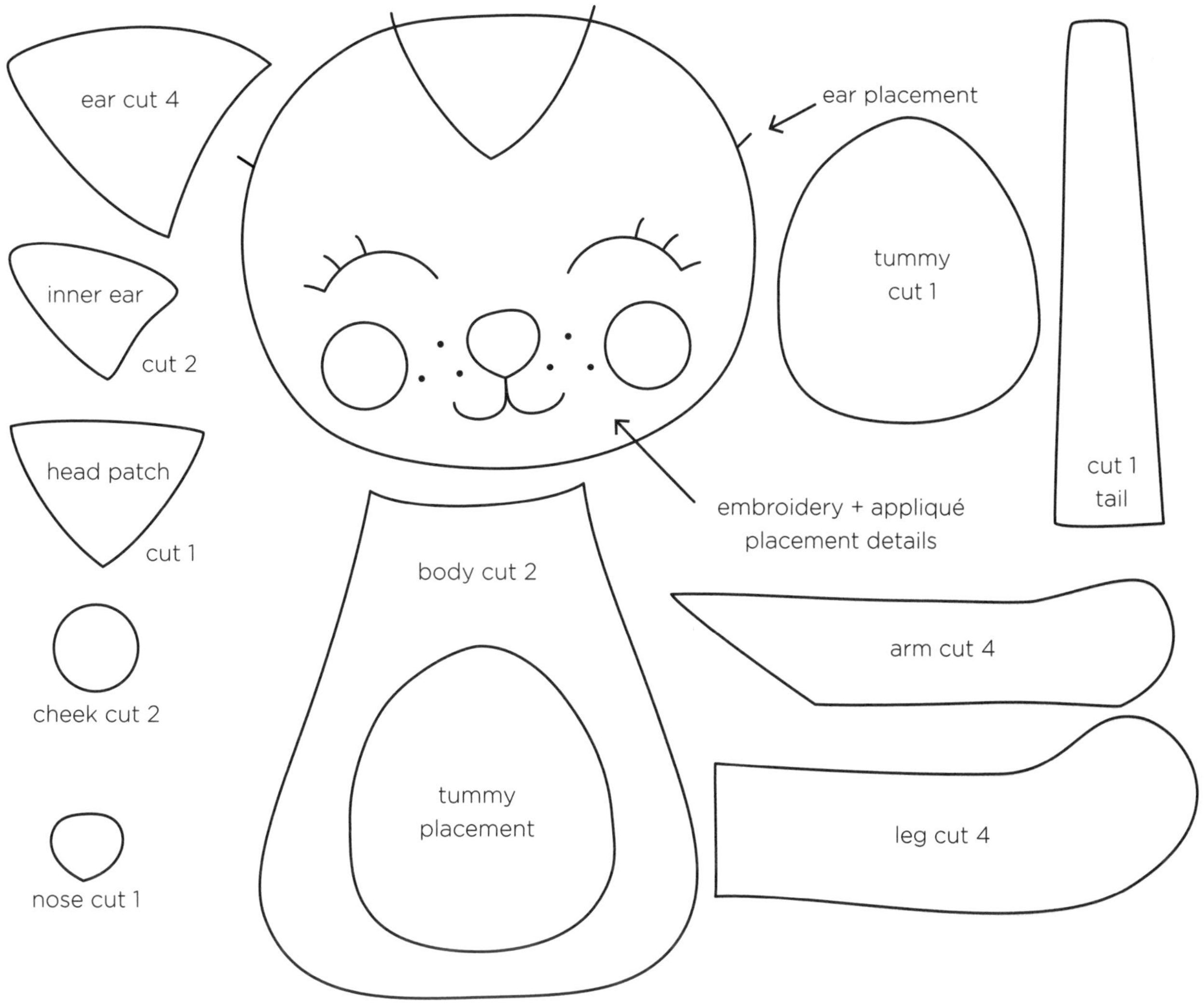
ear cut 4
inner ear
cut 2
head patch
cut 1
cheek cut 2
nose cut 1
ear placement
tummy
cut 1
cut 1
tail
embroidery + appliqué
placement details
body cut 2
arm cut 4
tummy
placement
leg cut 4

Lovely Leaf
Scissor Keeper
Page 137

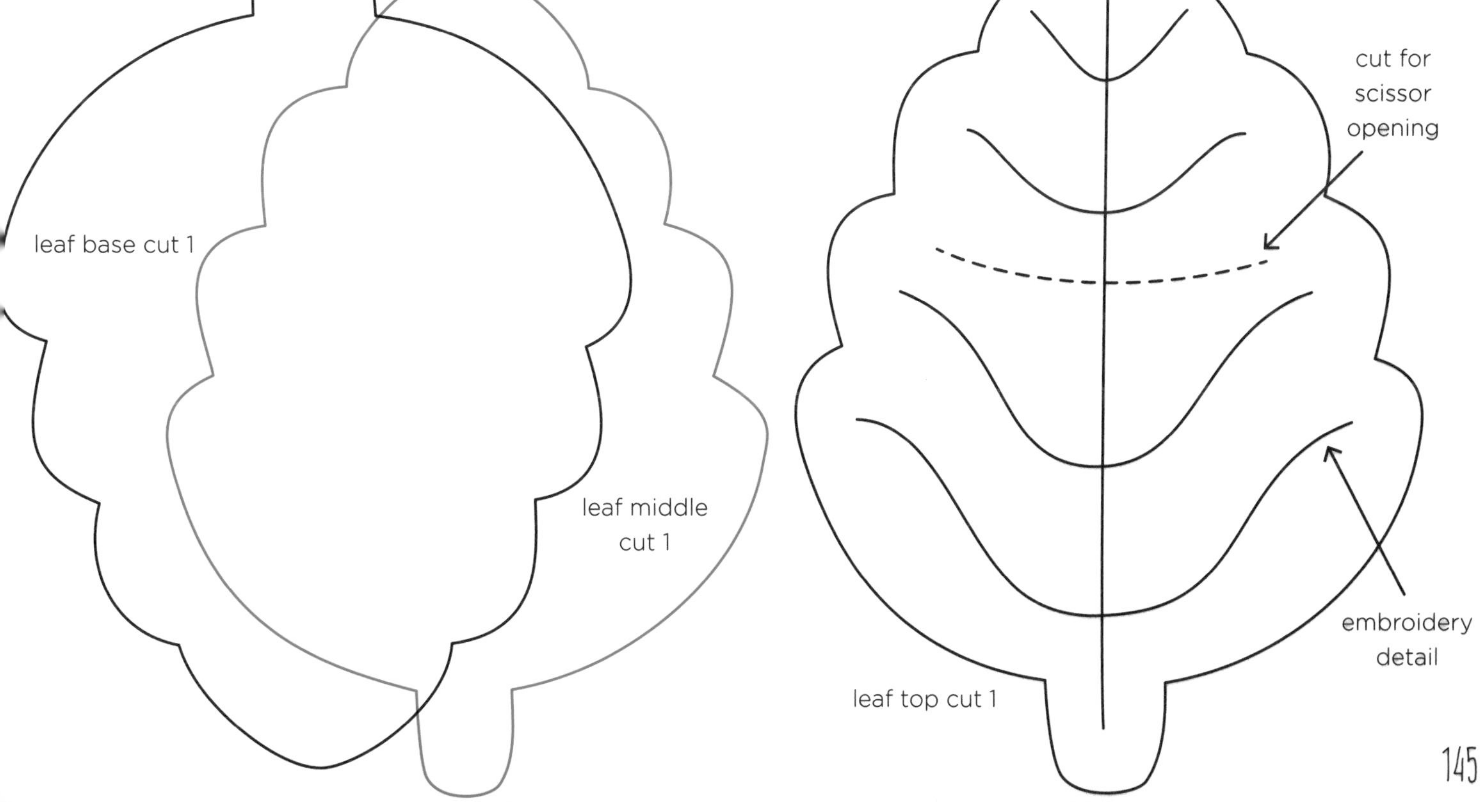
leaf base cut 1
leaf middle
cut 1
cut for
scissor
opening
embroidery
detail
leaf top cut 1

rolled centre template

flower template

leaf template 1

leaf centre
template

leaf
template 2

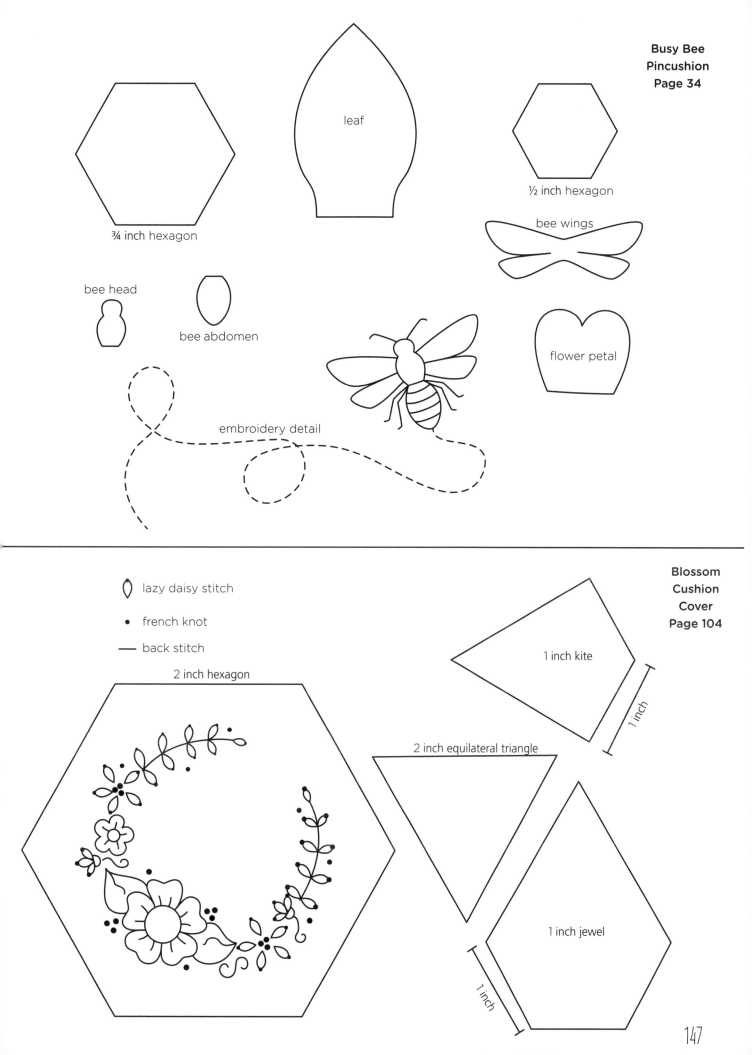

¾ inch hexagon

leaf

½ inch hexagon

bee wings

bee head

bee abdomen

flower petal

embroidery detail

lazy daisy stitch

french knot

back stitch

2 inch hexagon

1 inch kite

1 inch

2 inch equilateral triangle

1 inch jewel

1 inch

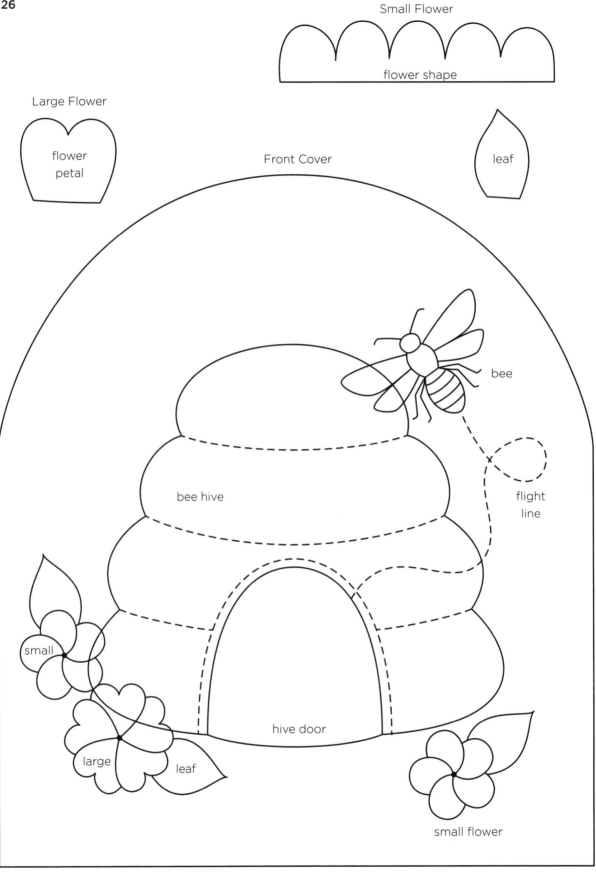

Small Flower

flower shape

Large Flower

flower petal

Front Cover

leaf

bee

flight line

bee hive

small

large

leaf

hive door

small flower

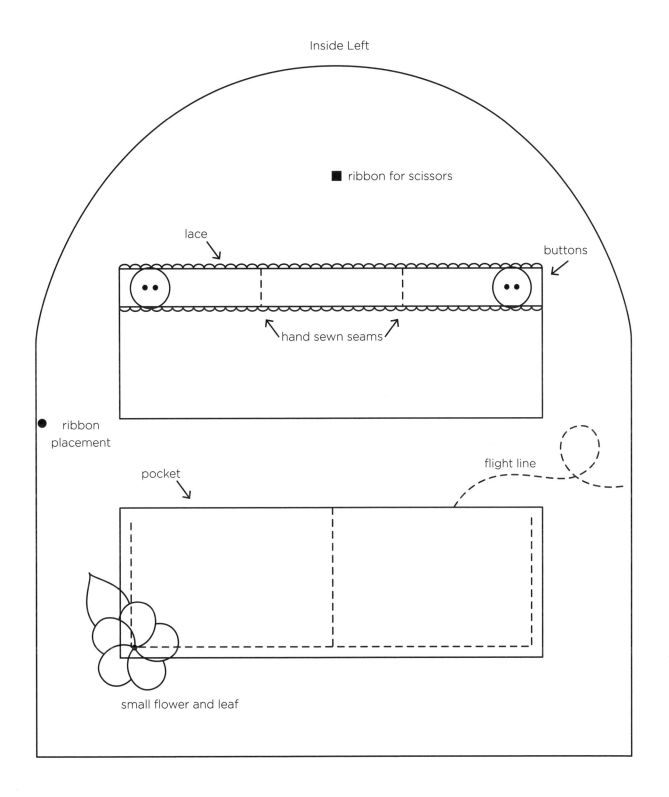

Inside Left

ribbon for scissors

lace

buttons

hand sewn seams

ribbon
placement

flight line

pocket

small flower and leaf

Inside Right

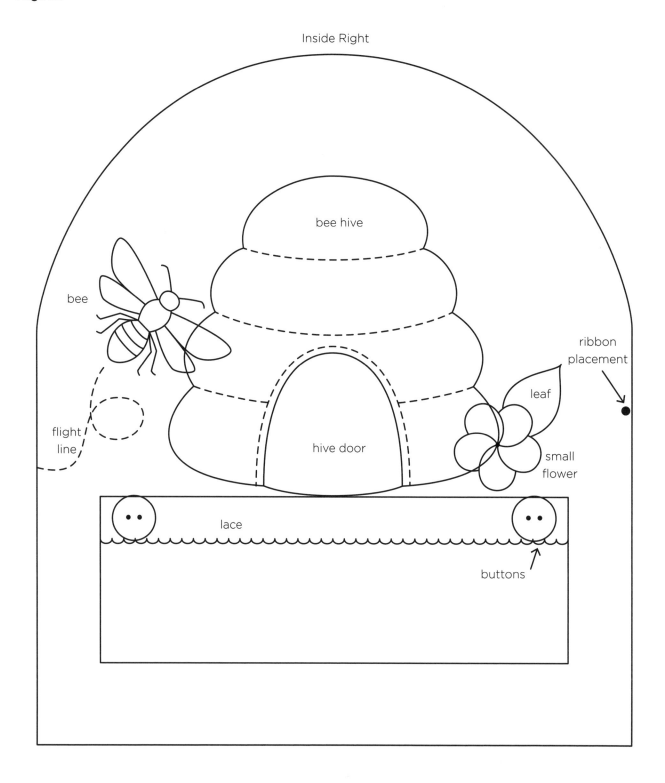

bee hive

bee

ribbon
placement

leaf

flight
line

small
flower

hive door

lace

buttons

Back Cover

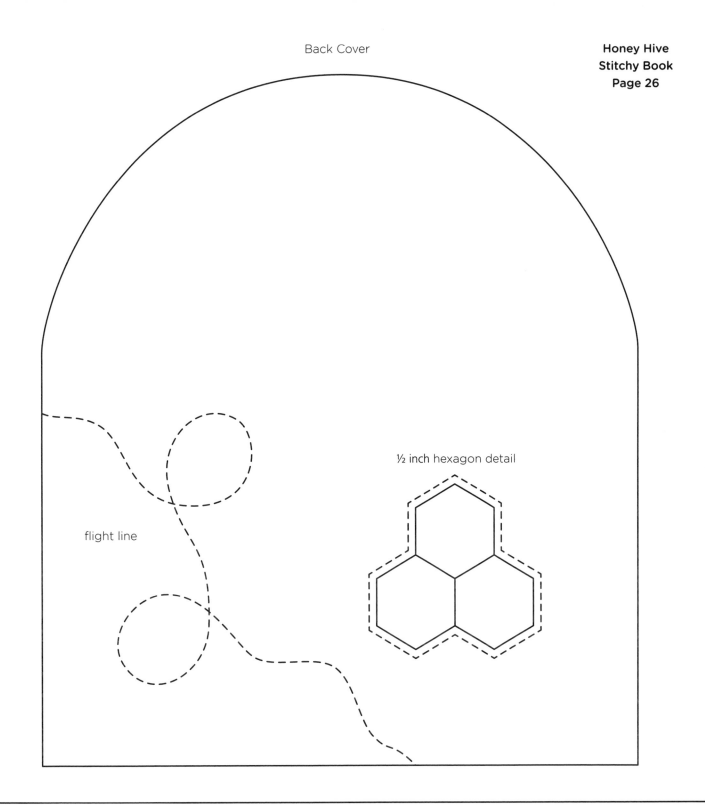

½ inch hexagon detail

flight line

**Posie
Patchwork Pouch
Page 92**

flower cut 2

flower
centre

cut 2

leaf
cut 2

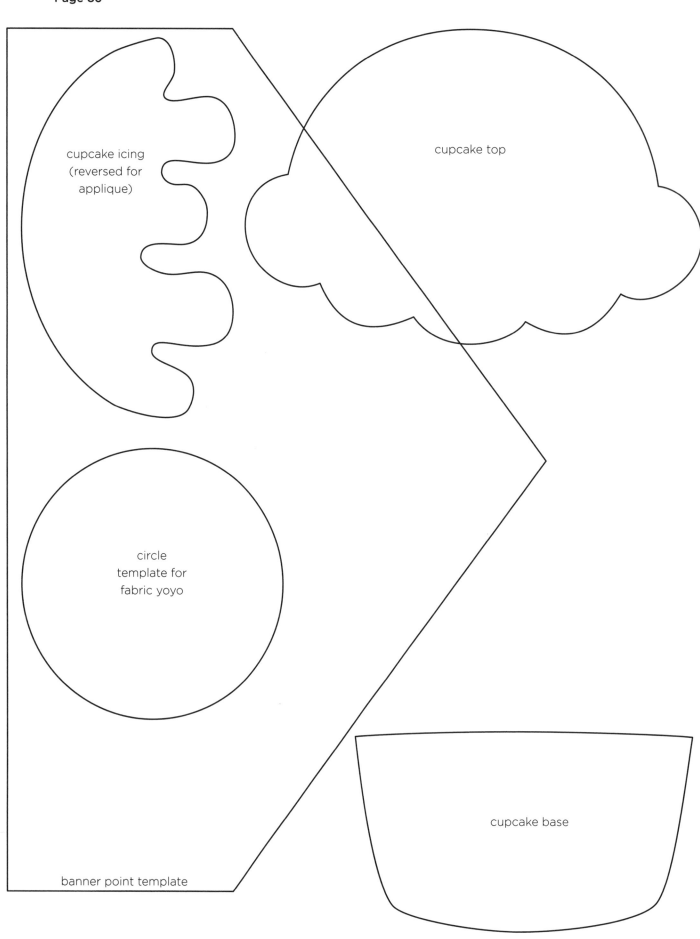

cupcake icing
(reversed for
applique)

cupcake top

circle
template for
fabric yoyo

cupcake base

banner point template

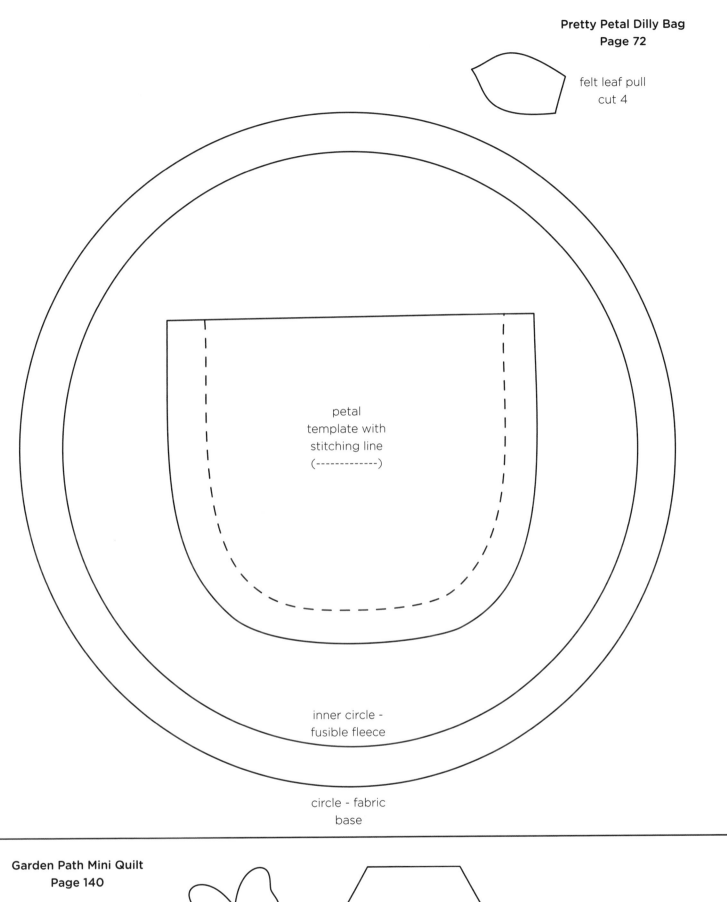

felt leaf pull
cut 4

petal
template with
stitching line
(-------------)

inner circle -
fusible fleece

circle - fabric
base

Garden Path Mini Quilt
Page 140

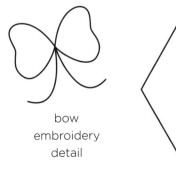

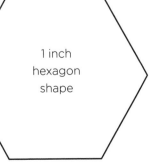

1 inch
hexagon
shape

bow
embroidery
detail

pincushion
base and top
cut 2

leaf shape

hair shape cut 1

Peach
Petunia
flower cut 1

hair
placement

face
shape
cut 1

embroidery
detail

pincushion
side
cut 1

Pink Peony
middle flower
cut 1

Pink Peony
outer flower
cut 1

Pink Peony
inner flower
cut 1

Susie
Sunflower
cut 2

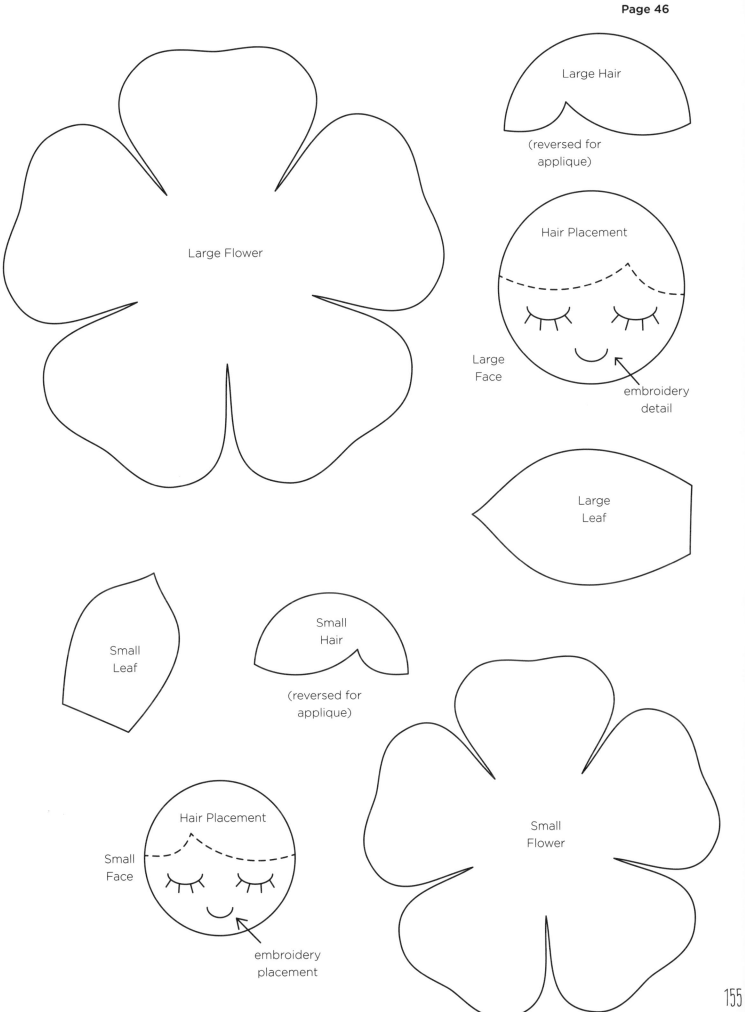

Large Hair

(reversed for applique)

Hair Placement

Large Flower

Large Face

embroidery detail

Large Leaf

Small Leaf

Small Hair

(reversed for applique)

Small Flower

Hair Placement

Small Face

embroidery placement

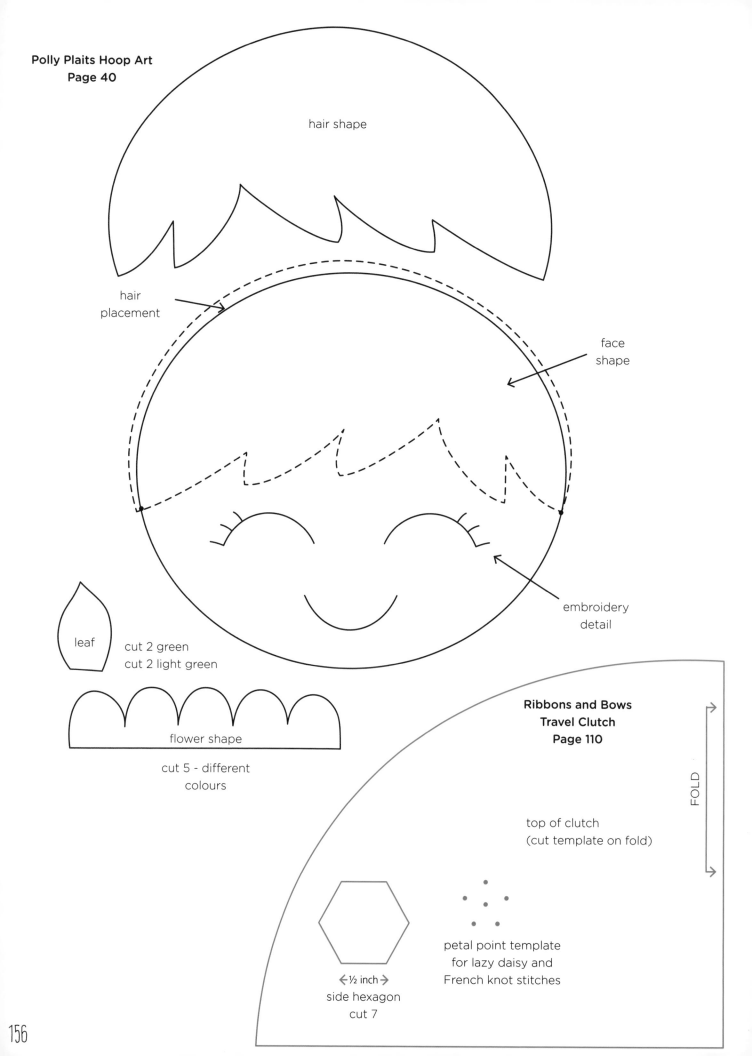

**Polly Plaits Hoop Art
Page 40**

hair shape

hair placement

face shape

embroidery detail

leaf

cut 2 green
cut 2 light green

flower shape

cut 5 - different colours

**Ribbons and Bows
Travel Clutch
Page 110**

FOLD

top of clutch
(cut template on fold)

petal point template
for lazy daisy and
French knot stitches

← ½ inch →
side hexagon
cut 7

flower appliqué shape

flower centre cut 2

felt flower cut 2

strawberry appliqué shapes for back cover

top appliqué shape

felt strawberry cut 2

(reversed for appliqué)

strawberry appliqué shape

French knots

felt strawberry top cut 2

Strawberry Surprise
Journal Cover
Page 122

Strawberry Surprise
Bookmark
Page 128

embroidery design

Diary

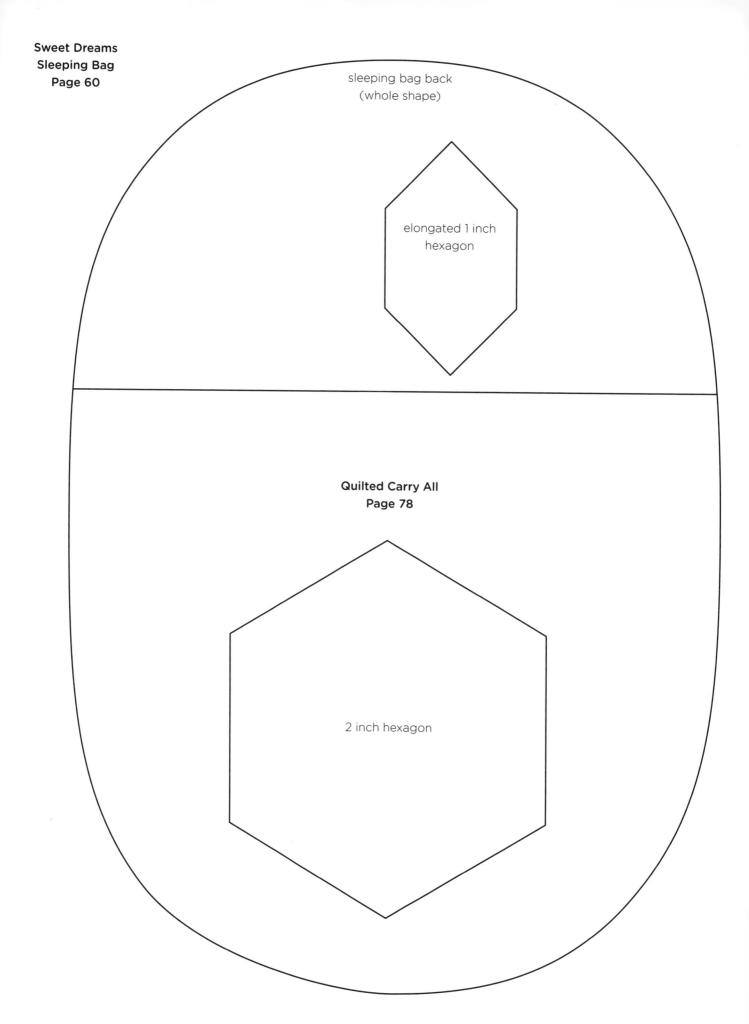

**Sweet Dreams
Sleeping Bag
Page 60**

sleeping bag back
(whole shape)

elongated 1 inch
hexagon

**Quilted Carry All
Page 78**

2 inch hexagon

icing

cupcake pieces
reversed for
appliqué

top

cupcake
placement

base

tea pot
placement

lid

band

spout

pot

handle

tea pot pieces
reversed for
appliqué

cream

cake slice pieces
reversed for
appliqué

icing

cake slice placement

side

side strip

tea cup
placement

mouth

band

tea cup pieces reversed for
appliqué

saucer

cup

handle